In God We Trust

In God We Trust

An American Experience

Ike C. Udeh

Rev. date: 08/04/2017

To order additional copies of this book, contact:
Xlibris
1-888-795-4274
www.Xlibris.com
Orders@Xlibris.com
765143

CONTENTS

Chapter I: Tales of Splendor...1

Chapter II: A Changing Person 26

Chapter III: The Way It Was 34

Chapter IV: What the System Has for You 45

PART TWO

Chapter V: A World View..69

Chapter VI: Limitations 86

Chapter VII: Working with the System 104

Chapter VIII: The People You Meet 121

Chapter IX: The Transformation 132

Chapter X: In God We Trust 147

About the Author 159

Outlined and composed in Cambridge, Massachusetts, twenty-five to thirty years ago; expanded in San Francisco; and subsequently completed in Silicon Valley, California.

Ike C Udeh
Palo Alto, California

For God,
humanity, and
the mystery of *nothing*

CHAPTER I

Tales of Splendor

THE TRAVELER COULD hear the clamor. He could hear the name and the words that tell of a place so beautiful, yet so structured and maddeningly driven that some could even feel the resplendence, so palpable and real that its very mention seems to beckon and invite anyone to its shores. He could sense its greatness, its distinction, and its pluralistic communities, which accommodate every being and every soul from all the corners of the earth. The traveler could sense all this from all the tales, told by various people around the globe and filtered through every peephole or cave a million miles away.

He even wonders if what he hears is real but doesn't exactly doubt or outright entertain the validity of the tales he's heard from those who have been there. But he could grasp the insistence that typifies the statement of those who had been there as they claim that what they say is true. These words, from those with firsthand experience, seem to make anyone hunger for a taste of what he or she has heard about this exceptionally different place of human dwelling.

It is such that as you go from place to place, the story takes its form, often augmented by the teller's own perception and some personal experience that could detract or embellish, depending on what predominant factors play as antecedents in the teller's experience.

Could this be America? And what some people hear from a million miles away sways their inclinations and shifts their minds toward a different kind of thought process. Gradually, they begin to buy into most of what they've heard, and a quiet yearning for what they think could be a wonderful experience begins to build in their minds.

It appears these tales about this rather otherworldly kind of place called America often have very strong influences on any culture they touch, and in most countries, the host culture begins to suffer. In time, the very basic fabrics that form the fundamental structure of the culture begin to weaken as the citizens gradually adjust their perceptions of their own culture to accommodate what they now feel is a better culture. As this process continues, the guardians of the host culture take steps to protect their own and insulate it from what they may consider contamination by an alien culture. In some countries, carefully crafted elements of protection are legislated into the system and what are considered protective restraints are planned into place. Some would even go as far as having neighbors spy on neighbors and encourage them to report any instance of a wavering mind who might be inclined to dream of this distant place, this community, the Land of Freedom in which everyone is supposedly equal and everyone can achieve his fullest potential.

In spite of such gallant efforts, however, the people yearn and dream. They plan and search for ways to beat the system and go for their dreams. Even the culture itself appears to bend of its own accord to the whims of the invading American culture.

And the traveler has often heard it said that in whichever society you dwell, you could sense the evident clash of principles, practices, and the trend of individual predilections. You could see the obvious strength of each culture, the American and the domestic. But you can sense the beginning of a sad requiem, which presages the demise of the domestic culture. But as an individual who's lived all his life in a particular place, you have a definite stake in whatever goes on in your society. You feel you are a part of the community and you are aware of the mental and physical investments you've made in the principles of your culture; and as such, the invasion by this supposedly better American culture begins to threaten your otherwise reasoned perspectives on life and society. And from his perspective, the traveler feels that everyone has an attachment to the culture in which he was born.

You probably saw the wholesomeness of your culture and experienced its nurturing concept. You appreciated the benefits that lay in its goodness, and since that was the only culture you knew so well, you probably developed a strong adherence to its principles and felt strongly about the necessity for every citizen to uphold these principles.

For some, this feeling of cultural and social responsibility becomes a very necessary obligation sustained by strong emotions. There may not be anything really wrong with this mind-set, except in cases when its application to common everyday occurrences becomes such a must-do undertaking that it begins to override the need for a reasoned approach to social/cultural demands.

In most cultures, there are those people who accept without critical analysis every word or gospel their culture preaches. For such people, there is a blind adherence to the principles of the culture, and this is often couched on a mind-set of total acceptance and subservient submission to the demands of the culture. Incidentally, some of these demands are perceived demands created by the individual to lend justification to his narrowly defined criteria for being an honest citizen, one whose patriotic stance on matters of state and country entertains no room for debate. It is often such people who have a very difficult time when confronted with the prospects of seeing the shift in their own culture as an alien culture invades their community.

But for most people, in time, as an alien culture, albeit one that toots its horn so loudly, continues to invade their community, they begin to question some of the previously accepted principles of their own culture. They gradually find themselves at odds with the fundamental basis of their own beliefs. Their otherwise firmly grounded position within their environment beings to seem precarious. Some of their social inclinations, previously wholeheartedly accepted, find them at a crossroads. They feel there is no in- between, no room broad enough to mentally accommodate what has been inculcated in them and what they now face.

In their quandary, however, these people still feel a certain sense of ownership about their culture since, apparently, this residual emotion and sense of belonging leave them with a feeling of pride. It also sustains their mental state as a bold affirmation of their person.

Invariably, in time, the reassessment of the culture and what it stood for by the individual proceeds faster than he expected, because this thing about this alien culture, which is supposedly perfect, has a very strong pull on him and most of the people around him. Perhaps the individual does not exactly dismiss his culture totally, but he now yearns for another one, which he is encouraged to believe is better. This person is, at this point, emerging from the crossroads at which he found himself at the initial stages; and working through personal reassessments, he begins to seek comfortable grounds from which he could launch his plans and decide which way to go.

As it often happens, the forces of the invading culture get increasingly stronger and the impact on the individual's mental disposition gets stronger as well. It is worth noting that this could be you within your society; this is you within the familiar confines of your own culture, and this is you struggling with critical decisions, which could effectively change your life. You may wonder then how much of an emotional struggle awaits you when you finally decide to relocate and leave all that you've known behind. When you do relocate to America, it may not be simply the familiarity of your previous culture that you leave behind but also the comfort, the safety, and the accommodating environment, which felt nurturing and nonthreatening to your existence.

For some, a decision to leave their place of birth and relocate in a foreign land seems to come relatively easy and any doubts and fear of the unknown are mediated by the excitement and exuberance generated by the belief in the apparent abundance of possibilities there are in the foreign place in which they've decided to relocate. For these, the pull from the stories they've heard about this foreign place is total and their belief in everything they heard is absolute. Of course, in some cases, the decision to pack up and relocate is encouraged by difficult conditions, which made life miserable in their own country.

Even among this set of easy converts, there are those who find themselves in dire situations after they relocate. From the moment they arrive in America, they are greeted by the glitter, the seemingly excessive luminance, and the maddening ubiquity of flashing lights from a million neon signs, which vie for saliency as they push the various items posted for public consumption. They notice the unending rush and jostling as masses of humanity compete for space and fight for opportunity. For these new arrivals in America, the scene becomes threatening, intolerant, and rather hostile. They begin to wonder why they chose to relocate in the first place.

Some among these new arrivals actually pack up and head back to where they came from. Some can't bear the thought of having to explain to their folks why they decided to return home, so they try to stick it out. You may not be among this group of settlers who decide to pack up and go back home, but as a new arrival, this rather nascent experience becomes one of several that presage the difficulties that lay ahead. Along with the pleasures, successes and, possibly, riches, which may come your way, there could be various issues, personal and social, you have to deal with.

It is fair to say that among these various issues, some difficult and some not terribly demanding, lie instances of opportunity that, seized in time, could pave the way for ultimate success.

As you begin to wade into the demands of everyday living in America, you find yourself seeking solutions to a multitude of questions seemingly without answers. You begin to realize what the culture entails as the inner workings are revealed. Before you arrived in America, most of the tales you heard often painted a beautiful picture of a scene with no blemishes, at least not like the culture you lived in or any other place. But as you begin to settle in whatever neighborhood you've chosen to live in, the reality of life as it is lived in American society begins to awaken your sense of caution and a tempered feeling of excitement. And, yes, there is still some excitement and a feeling of joy. After all, this is America. This is the seat of human freedom unlike any other place. But this feeling of joy and excitement is tempered by a restrained sense of appreciation, as some aspects of the culture in their practical applications appear to contradict the intended meaning of the basic letters in the stated definition of freedom.

In comparison with your mind-set before you decided to relocate, your thoughts are now plagued by a rather different perspective. The picture is taking a very different form, and you are faced with various issues—some of them disconcerting at best and maddeningly conflicting at worse. They conflict with what you knew and accepted as primary determinants of an amicable coexistence among humans in a human society. As you go about your business and try to fit into your new community, you may find that some of the issues, mostly social, which you have to deal with, seem to be beyond the readily available processes of simple resolution. But you are now in America, and you have decided to stay; and this decision to stick it out in the face of irresolvable issues awakens the need for a reassessment of self, safety, and success. In this process of reassessment, you realize that you, your being, and the very essence of your personhood now need a newer and perhaps reconsidered articulation to help you settle in your new society.

As a transplant in America, one of the things you learn early is that it is a society on a fast track—a very fast track that always reminds you that the society does not wait for anyone. With this knowledge, you seek to find your cue and march along with everyone else. As for the difficult social issues and the rather differently strange cultural factors, you try to categorize them and subsequently place them in a compartmentalized set of factors worthy of temporary suspension.

And so, you begin to feel a sense of mixed emotions. You watch, either in dismay or excitement, as your mind begins to grapple with what appears to be a resolution to some of the questions plaguing your thoughts. And with this sense of resolution, you begin to feel like you are approaching a definite stance as you begin to find the room for the accommodation and acceptance of your new society, perhaps not exactly for its less convincing aspects but for the sheer attraction of its novelty and promises.

As you seek to accommodate these initial issues and begin to settle mentally, there is a latent feeling of safety and some personal comfort. Because such a feeling of safety helped to ground and anchor your being in your previous society, you are naturally inclined to accept and want more of those factors, which make your new society work.

So as you toil and seek to find your path in this frenzied track of human race for survival, you play it deftly—you work with the dictates of the culture for survival—but you still hold on to some of the principles of the old culture for mental soundness, at least until you feel sufficiently safe and settled in the new society. Ultimately, you feel satisfied that there was no intent, you do not question the authenticity of the culture you left behind; you did not dismiss its validity or trivialize the benefits, which lay in its applicability within its own confines. And incidentally, a latent sense of nostalgia inexorably elevates these benefits, perhaps a notch beyond their worth, but worthy nonetheless.

But as you begin to find your niche in your newly adopted American society, you begin to discard some of the previously held views of your old culture. The longer you remain in America, the more you find reason for that aspect of the system you initially felt was unreasonable; and you find accommodation for that which you considered unacceptable. Your mind-set begins to find you at a point of convergence at which the old finds the new, and invariably, something begins to give. The play and promise of the American culture, including the tantalizing presence of its seductive abundance, becomes stridently attractive. Perhaps the unexpected advantage here is that what you regarded in and about your old culture as an instance of universal acceptance becomes exposed only as good but essentially particular and not necessarily universally acceptable.

In substance, you'd lived your old culture all along by viewing the particular as universal and unquestionably beneficial to all humankind.

As a transplant in America, your next dilemma then may be precisely how not to jump on the bandwagon and join everyone else in putting down other cultures as no good and totally unfit for human existence. Some views even go so far as to define most other societies as primitive. But this should not be an issue for you since you will soon learn that everything *other* than American almost always gets more than one definition. And at times, these other instances or occasions get such a plethora of definitions that you are inclined only to opt for a more balanced approach; you view it all in perspective and place them in their proper context; ultimately, they play like any other human instance with merits and demerits, which, in the end, tells you it's all good!

Since every human culture has its ups and downs, that by definition includes the American culture. And similar to other human cultures, the American also has its downside. At this point, as a transplant, perhaps you could argue about which aspect outweighs the other. A cursory look into some of the advances, both in medicine and technology, leaves no doubt about the culture's advancement and greatness. In some aspects, particularly science, it's simply amazing. In the field of medicine, some of the work is almost impossible to grasp, and of course, that too happens to be one of the more appealing factors that piqued your curiosity and encouraged you to relocate.

Of course, in spite of it all, in spite of the almost magic of science and medicine and every other great idea, people still die. Oh yes, like in every other human society, people die here too. And like every other human society, death does unearth some of humanity's rather unsavory inclinations. Here, in America, it is no different. Witness the rush with which the bereaved go for whatever the dead left behind! You are inclined to wonder how much they wished the poor fellow would pass sooner than he did. This behavior may not necessarily be because they want to loot what he left but also because the people are in a mad rush to get whatever they can and proceed as quickly as possible to enjoy the loot. They have to act this way, of course, because the dead fellow's death did not only provide them with instant wealth but also mirrors and affirms their own fate, and this they see, irrespective of age, is just around the corner. So, it seems, the unspoken but very well-understood statement here is "Oh yes, he's dead, very dead! Quick, check out whatever he left besides the bills and grab whatever you can. We'll tell him what we did with his toys and loot when we join him!" But don't let this cultural phenomenon disturb your mind, for it is one of those very American practices you will soon be admiring. Let's face it, what's so wrong with joining a mad rush for a dead man's loot when you know damn well how difficult it is to land any free goodies?

At this point of your stay in your new society, chances are you've become quite adept at juxtaposing one item of discourse with other. You find reason for the seemingly unreasonable, and you entertain some not-so-convincing ideas as long as they serve to lend credence to your inclinations. You are beginning to view yourself as a potential success. After all, what this culture has always preached is that no matter who you are, no matter what your religious affiliations are, and no matter how much effort you need to go from point A to B, you can succeed. In substance, you are told you are a person, you are human, you can succeed, and the sky is the limit!

Your decision, however, is no different than that of most of your predecessors who felt there was a definite potential for betterment and decided to relocate to America. Perhaps you suspect something a little daring about those people who were the very first transplants, who dared to leave that which they knew so well and that which had raised and bred them. But as you proceed to find your niche in America, how your predecessors came and what motivated their move becomes less significant. You probably can only relate and admire that which stands out about their action.

These people, some from the same place as you, did more than believe absolutely in what they heard about the American culture. They dared to dream and venture beyond the familiar confines of their place of birth. And since the substance of their dreams played in concert with the tantalizing tales of America and its promises, the country beckoned with irresistible opportunities predicated on absolute human freedom.

Now you take success, blend it with abundance, and top it off with absolute freedom—it's stupendously tempting and simply irresistible!

So as you run around trying to find your place and eventually make it in America, you remain aware that, yes, you are no different from everyone else who left his place of birth and relocated here. And as the demands of American life and the trend of some rather difficult social issues dog every one of your steps, you become very aware that this is your time, your play, and your business. And whatever be your chosen occupation, it is explicitly your responsibility to find your way as you fashion your personal dance through the maze of the unique American social system. As you probably have learned, there are no in-betweens. You work with what you've got to keep what you've got and interact with reason within the bounds of realism. You find little or no room for pretenses but ample room for the concrete realization of your dreams.

As your daily activities begin to broaden, you find no room for vacillation and indecision. Most of the seemingly disparate factors, which initially greeted you on arrival, appear to act in concert with your activities as they seemingly pull themselves into a consortium of not-so-salient elements, which vie for consideration from just beneath the surface of your conscious mind.

But you are still quite new in America and just beginning to figure out how to find your place. In your spare moments, however, it is possible that your mind still wrestles with various issues regarding your previous community, such as the family, the scene, relatives, your friends, and your previous home. And some of these issues may relate to some previously unimportant things like the neighbor back home who everyone in the neighborhood considered a social isolate and, consequently, weird and a little nutty; but now he becomes rather significant in your thoughts.

This person comes into focus now because his lifestyle back there is very similar to what you are experiencing as the norm in America. The face and style of this person's life immediately commands your mind's attention, and this immediacy suggests a reconsideration of a lifestyle you probably once deemed crazy. You may not be totally amazed by this experience of a profound difference in what is culturally and socially acceptable between the two cultures, but since the basis of your ideas still has its roots in your previous culture, the need to feel comfortable in your new culture propels you to find a synthesis. So you invariably search for a common ground as your inclinations sift through different ways of coordinating the varying cultural elements into sequential clusters of meaningful ideas.

Perhaps you rest with the thought that what obtained back home is valid and significant, and its validity and significance are predicated on its utility as demonstrated by the benefits derived from its social application. In this case, a lifestyle that was viewed as odd in one culture seems quite okay and viewed only as different in another. Perhaps, in your previous culture, like in most others, a lifestyle that seemed to display a departure from the norm was viewed with some doubts as to its validity. But it still remained a part of the variety within the community.

And, by the way, the same holds true in America.

You begin to notice quite a sizable number of activities played out differently in America than in your old society. The very imposing presence of structures around you is obvious. The pace is very different, and contrary to some of the tales you heard, the folks here don't exactly drift effortlessly through the air; they don't run around picking pennies off the ground and having wealth and abundance drift into their pockets. You notice the rush, however, for this is the perennial American virtue, and you sense the ever-present air of highly competitive existence. Perhaps some of the tales you heard painted a picture of a superlatively enlightened instance of amicable human interaction. Some of those tales even told of a superhuman achievement of successfully banishing death and the constraints of death from the society.

But, you wonder, is this really possible?

While your mind places this death-defying feature of the society in limbo until you see the proof thereof, you feel there is a disconcerting absence of true human relationship. Perhaps a tiny voice from the back of your mind thinks, "Well, if these folks can make it a death-free society, who needs true relationship? Who needs this stuff if we are all going to live forever?

But you wonder nonetheless if the prospects of living forever are truly desirable; after all, the prospects of seeing your cantankerous neighbor and your ex-partner forever would be so boring that folks would go somewhere else to kick the bucket, not necessarily to rest in peace but to permanently rest from the neighbor's harassment and the partner's unending demand for support and attention.

Oh yes, this is America!

And, damn it, it's all human!

As you wonder about what else can be there behind the scenes that makes this truly a different kind of human environment, you witness the antagonism and the pretentious smile that mark the various person-to-person relationships. You also notice that amid the wealth and plenty, there is a sizable number of those who can hardly afford one meal a day. And along with the abundant wealth, there is a remarkable abundance of those who constitute what is socially classified as the homeless. You watch as these folks amble around and shuffle from place to place with all they possess while those who enjoy the abundance rush past in their constant rush and search for toys. Then, something reminds you of a statement you've heard the residents make— "It's dog eat dog"— and this puts everything into proper context. So now that you are in America and a part of the society, the question becomes not so much how you can make it as which dog you can eat before you get eaten.

So before you really settle in your new world and before you actually find a permanent niche, you are already thinking differently than you previously did. And just in case you are tempted to entertain any thoughts of being different, well, you may want to go it slow, for you are fast becoming like everyone else an intrinsic part of the community. If you thought the residents think and act like animals, same goes for you. And as animals, perhaps you are, like everyone else, only slightly fortunate that you are bipedal, the incidence of bipedalism only slightly distinguishing you and your human neighbors from the four-legged ones. Or does it really? At least in the animal world, there is an accepted form of social behavior and conduct. You kill to satisfy your hunger. You drink to quench your thirst. You adhere to a strict code of territoriality and clearly nuanced form of communication. You avoid waste, and you avoid the discomforts of its consequences. You dare to contrast that culture with that of your fellow humans; a sense of responsibility tinged with awe makes you shudder at the rate including the abandon with which humanity is destroying their only home, the planet. And ultimately, you wonder why it seems so natural that humans quite comfortably sanction the destruction of these four-legged creatures.

At this early stage of settlement, you are beginning to experience what the society truly has to offer. As the day-to-day activities play all around you, you witness life in practically all its forms. You see the various types who make up the population go about their business in what is fairly accurately termed *to each his own*. You also witness how the different folks seek ways to transcend some of life's vicissitudes that come their way. The misfortunes of life appear to occur at every turn as some people can't help but watch their spirit flag and fall at the onset of misfortune.

It could feel somewhat disconcerting as you watch some of your fellow humans as they deal with some very pronounced difficulties of human existence that plague their person. If perhaps you felt back home that human existence was not an easy enterprise, now you feel it's not simply uneasy but almost a curse. You wonder whether the more advanced the society, the more complicated the human tragedy. In some instances, tragedies and misfortunes seem to diminish your presence and negate the very incidence of your being.

In your new American society, it appears the resident folks have decided to mediate some of the unpleasant aspects of life by acquiring as many toys as they can. As you run around trying to beat the clock of life, you can always kick back at the end of the day and let the sight of your acquisitions ameliorate the impact of life's difficulties. As a transplant, you may not have to worry about just how to fit your mind into this process, because soon enough you will find the reason, or the reason will find you and shape your views. You begin to see why you must make it at all cost; and you must be prepared—always—to flaunt the toys you've amassed, which not only soothe you but also define you socially. The toys, it is said, are also designed to uplift you and place you a tad above your less fortunate neighbor. So even in your very private moments, when you have only your mind to listen to, you are encouraged to look around and savor the moment by admiring the soothing presence of your toys.

Some would swear this experience is magical. But, you guessed it, it depends on the individual. After all, folks have been known to swear that they don't exactly look at their toys and insist that their toys have a way of looking at them. And this unique experience gives them the greatest joy. However, you need not be alarmed by the tales of these persons with rather distinguished experience. They are the lucky few with a different view of things. And just in case you are tempted to jump to conclusions and consider them crazy, you may need to hold off a little. After all, this is America; whether you are looking at your toys, or your toys are looking at you, it's all OK.

IKE C. UDEH

Perhaps, at this point, you are beginning to get the picture. In American society, you must have toys whether you need them or want them. The culture preaches it. The system mandates it. Anything short of this makes you something of a misfit.

In order to acquire these toys, you join the race and take your turn from the queue in a maddening process of breakneck competition. The pace gets so fast that at times you feel you have no time to even think. The preferred style is dehumanizing. The process, uncompromising. Occasionally, the thought drifts through your mind that this is what you journeyed for. But you can't lose hope because you dare not—you are considered a failure if you do! And since the essence of life in America is sustained competition, you'd better be always prepared to compete.

When you do find the moment to assess how well you've done so far and analyze any changes in your views regarding your new society, you may find that you are being less dismissive of any aspects of the culture. You are beginning to see this as life at its ultimate. It is life as perhaps never seen before. It is a pluralistic environ of human subjects, a social experiment that promises to elevate your whole life and secure your place as a human being beyond the realms of all other creatures.

At this point, you begin to appreciate some of the apparent wonders of human achievements—some of them almost impossible to comprehend and some seemingly magical in their operation. This is truly a human experiment in which the experimenter becomes his own subject for experiment. You find the tool for every job and the job for every tool.

As you get more engrossed in whatever occupies your time, you barely realize how much your whole being is wrapped up by your preoccupations. Invariably, you fail to notice that no sooner you begin to play your part in the whole system than you are contributing to those processes that are very critical in maintaining the fundamental principles of this social system.

In a not-too-frequent moment of self-evaluation, you find that consciously and, at times, subconsciously, you've embarked on a process of fitting in. You proceed to craft your own niche within a complex web of a variety of social structures and individual predilections. You watch the various persons around you, both within your neighborhood and beyond, and notice the degree of determined individuality. It may not occur to you that this behavior could be mirroring a picture of you as your assimilation proceeds in full swing. You are just about finding your cue and set to compete. You feel it is just fine for you to hustle and, like everyone else around you, begin to gather as many toys as you can.

But every once in a while, as you hustle, you may be compelled by the forces of negation to stop and reexamine your activities particularly when, despite all your struggles, you find you have very little of substance to show for it. Now you are inclined to evaluate your choices and try to reexamine your order of preference and validate its utility. At this point, you are probably still inclined to view and do things in the manner you did when you were back home, which means that in some situations, you'd look at things differently than the folks do in America. And because the problems you are dealing with are essentially different than the ones you experienced back home, you may be inclined, every so often, to wonder if your goals are not only proper but also appropriately defined to be accommodated by your capabilities. For some transplants, the ability to reassess their goals and evaluate their preferences occasionally provides the opportunity to get a clearer view of their decisions regarding their chosen line of business. It also provides them with the opportunity to review their responses to the demands of social responsibilities and helps them to stay on cue as they strive to retain their own space within the scheme of the social structure. These transplants appear to be gaining the grasp of what constitutes personal roles within the society and seem to appreciate the need for each person to play his part. As they strive to focus on their activities, they are being bombarded by novel experiences, unfamiliar cultural practices, and other environmental factors that impinge upon their senses. Along with this comes the need to remain focused while maintaining a good sense of judgment and the understanding of what it takes to maintain good health. These demands—some personal, mostly social—to these transplants are some of those aspects of the American culture the individual must meet. Meeting them, however, requires a conscious application of oneself. For the resident folks, this activity comes much easier as part of the familial and natural growing process; for the transplant, it comes a little harder as part of a new and often different learning process. The transplant often realizes this and proceeds to take the necessary steps.

You can only do this, however, assuming your mental disposition is still sound. People have been known to lose some of the critical functions of their senses, particularly in the early stages of their arrival in America, when problems they never imagined plague their minds. With regard to these, as well, it all becomes part of the unique American experience.

As a transplant in America, it may be prudent for the individual to retain some of his old views regarding person-to-person interactions. This could prove to be a particularly wise decision since interpersonal relationships, in most cases, are rather shallow, often transient, and based on material gains. But you will often find it necessary to work at not being taken for a ride, because it goes with the system to only give in accord with what you get. Some of the tales you heard initially about the society—some almost magical, some seemingly mythical, and others beyond simple comprehension—begin to either make sense or lose their appeal in contrast with the reality of actual interpersonal relationships.

Luck could be on your side if you find an honest and dependable relationship that is mutually respectful and equally considerate and caring. Relationships such as these can certainly be found in the American society, and some people have been exceptionally lucky to have found one that not only works for them but also helps them mentally and emotionally as they struggle to make it professionally, socially, and personally. For some, the demands from their professional endeavors and other activities often clash with the demands from the personal relationship, particularly the romantic relationship. This situation could be so pronounced that the individual finds himself doubting every one of his endeavors; he begins to question the benefits of his romance and doubt its utility and apparent necessity.

As you participate in the daily activities of your new society, you find that doubts and difficult issues, including incidents that seem to negate your existence, are factors that dog everybody in the American society. But people resort to various ways of handling their problems and dealing with these issues. Perhaps the more interesting choice, preferred by a good number of people, is to find nature and its inherent beauties.

You let your mind relax, and you notice the instances of splendor quietly announced by the very simple things around you such as the plants, the flowers, and the trees. You take in the skies, the streams, and the waters. You feel the air, soothing and refreshing. The other creatures around you come into life as you watch the sudden rise and instant drop of a bird as it flutters, floats, and flies. You witness the seemingly careless play of its wings as it dances through the air and deftly dives into a tree. You also witness and appreciate shadows around you as they almost imperceptibly move with the sun on a relucent object.

Your mind appreciates and quietly assimilates.

Some folks, on the other hand, find time to go away. They successfully skip the next headache by leaving the scene. In the process, they take a break from the concrete structures, stoic, cold, and often depressingly confining. They escape from the clutter and maddening clatter of automobiles. These folks eventually find a place, perhaps far, far away from their usual locale in America. They find a different lifestyle, one that appears to suggest a very slow motion of temporal flux.

And the slow pace of everything around inclines them to notice and watch distant shadows and seemingly restless clusters of clouds as

> They play —
> They drift and they dance —
> They weave —
> They swirl and they sway —
> They rise —
> They flow, and they fall —

And then they roam, separate and dissipate, poignantly reminding them and their humankind of the ephemerality of their preoccupations. And, yes, the futility and emptiness, so typical of most human endeavors, are particularly true in America.

Perhaps you happen to be one of those few who, after their arrival in America, don't feel very sure about what their life's endeavors are all about. But you are in a scene that stands as the ultimate in human endeavors, so you find company from among your kind: your neighbors, your friends, and all others, including, at times, your enemies.

Even if you are certain about what course you've set for your life and the substance of it, the sheer enormity of what constitutes life, including living in this society, entails a remarkable array of activities that constitutes a unique instance of human enterprise. The system in America has it all, including the best, the most alarming, the most impressive, and the most damnably abhorrent. You get the feeling anything within and seemingly beyond human capability is possible here. This feeling is further encouraged by the fact that there is every kind of mind from all parts of the globe here. And they all work in a disastrously competitive atmosphere but decidedly collaborative.

Which brings back the issue of banishing death from the American social scene. You probably did not believe this news when you first heard it, but you did not dismiss it outright. But as you watch the goings-on in your community, you witness evidence that seems to tell you otherwise. You see evidence of decay all around. You observe the infirm as they struggle just to place one foot in front of the other in order to walk. You hear about death, and you see death, sometimes quite close to you. And then you stop and wonder, as it appears that despite all the seemingly miraculous human endeavors, the frequency of death appears to rise in accord with the rise in sophistication.

Now you are beginning to see this thing about beating death as a myth probably planted in the social consciousness as a concept designed to elevate the spirit and minimize the ever-present threat of human mortality.

But then, you notice activities that aim to resurrect the dead and try to make him/her/it speak to the circumstances surrounding his death. You also see attempts at freezing the dead in order to bring him back sometime soon. In spite of all these activities, however, beating death, whether in America or anywhere else, still remains a myth. But is it really? As you may have noticed, or heard, there are plans at work through an interestingly captivating process within the high-tech sphere, appropriately termed *transhumanism*, etc., which seeks to somehow substitute a machine for your being. It seems, in its broader studies, a person can totally transcend the ordinary life and all its drawbacks, limitations, and constraints with the possibility of a forever existence. But then, you wonder, so what if another, with some rather nefarious intentions hacks into this "machine-being"? Could this character then bring about the end of this phenomenon? Perhaps you'd prefer not to bother with this rather different concept and stay with the current and basic process. It may seem rather simplistic and timeworn, but that remains part of its appeal as the simplistic element therein only plays in harmony with its ordinariness; it is common, it is general, and it is preordained: when there is life, there is death.

So it begins to dawn on you that this well-placed myth is only a confirmation of what you've always known—that your new world of America isn't necessarily different. The society simply has a way of dressing misfortune and repackaging human tragedy, which ultimately wraps it all up in a tidy package of not-so-overwhelming instances of human experience.

And your mind? It suggests, apparently, that you are in America. But are you really sure that is actually the case? Assurances could be confusing at times. But if that is truly the case, you may need to

Relax
And let your mind savor the moment

But as it is, you may not actually be in America. Your physical form only dwells in a void—your being is not exactly—and the very essence of your personhood lacks any practical specificity as testimony to an actual/real presence.

And this nudges the traveler's mind toward an attempt at disentangling the seemingly indefinable instance.

But there are no mysteries except to wonder, as the traveler appears to do, if yours, the very incidence of you, is a void; and no instance or occasion identifies or places you or your presence in a particular locality. Do you go through same human experience?

But being what it is, the nature of humans inclines you and others to place their persons in a practical, specific location at any given moment; it is a drive to accommodate the physical form in a particular point in place.

Are you in a quandary?

If so, or if not, precisely what kind of experience do you go through? The traveler may or may not be searching for answers.

At this point, as you savor the soothing presence of all you've acquired so far and watch the neighbors wallow in their wealth and dance amid the niceties of abundance, you wonder, what's all the fuss about? After all, it's all gonna be left behind ultimately!

The society, however, encourages you to get moving, and the system, with the sheer force of its seductive appeal, nudges you farther. In addition, as the successful neighbor gloats about his impressive collection of toys, you do a little hoot and holler and pretend that the miserable sight of your meager collection is actually worth more than it seems. Of course, this is your own secret; what you are really looking at is the potential from the perceived glories belying the promises of the future. Remarkably, in America, there is always the tantalizing sound, the appeal, and the seductively attractive occasion of success belying a promise of imminent material comfort. "You can make it," the system affirms. And besides, if everything else fails, you will *win the lottery*!

There may be times when a feeling of nostalgia brings back sharp memories of what you left back home, particularly those things that made you love your previous society and cherish the culture. At times such as these, you wonder if you've really made the right decision. And when the drag and constant demand from both personal and social responsibilities seem to wear you down mentally, you wish for a moment that you could give it all up and head back home. But no one really gives up acquired toys, including the ever-present prospect of acquiring more, only to head back to a place where his chances of making it seem very remote. Even the forces of greed, which invariably get a stranglehold on you, will make such a decision difficult to make. As you become more adept at dealing with these moments of nostalgia, you begin to feel more comfortable with the social demands and the dictates of the American culture. In the process, your once-critical mind broadens and gradually begins to accommodate some of those aspects of the culture you previously had difficulty accepting.

As you proceed to work your way toward establishing your own niche, you experience the different ways people in your new culture deal with some of the difficult problems that come their way every so often. At times, as you interact with others, you find that the differences in ways and methods of handling personal and/or social problems are quite remarkable. But before this phenomenon begins to alarm you, the neighbors will tell you it is the differences in personalities that account for it.

But the more you examine this instance of striking differences in personal approach to problems, the more interesting it gets. You may even find yourself wondering why there are so many problems in this society where there is a remarkable abundance of resources, including support and information.

Then you are forced to look closer and examine the issue, not really from an inordinately critical perspective but a fair and analytical one. You see, some people dive headlong into the contents of their problems and seek to find solutions as they wade through the rough currents. Some adopt a rather cautious approach and proceed in calculated steps as they tackle one issue after the other. And in this latter group, you find that the sheer applicability of their preferred method provides a measure of confidence that helps to sustain their drive and anchor their resolve.

You then wonder if the society has more to offer on this issue of how best to deal with problems both personal and social. But since this is a human community, something tells you there has to be more to it; and there's got to be some with a totally different approach to personal problems.

No sooner do you embark on further examination than you encounter others who handle things a lot differently than the previous ones you've seen. At the onset of problems, some of these simply watch things take their course and then seek handouts from the community or the state to help them solve their problems. You suspect that this group believes it is a personal right to be rescued by others in times of difficulties, and you wonder precisely what happens if nothing comes to them in the form of help or handout.

Since this is a multifaceted society that boasts a complete array of every type of personality, you still find some who simply do nothing but wallow in the difficulties of their problems, perceived or real, and mull endlessly over them. In the end, they pack up and depart for a different part of the community. These problem-induced relocations are often undertaken ostensibly to leave the scene and their problems behind. But it kind of gets a little sticky here, especially since personal problems do not exactly remain behind as you change locations. But don't tell that to these folks, or you'll find yourself quickly becoming the main cause of their problems.

Your examination of the various persons in the society and their different approaches to some of life's issues begins to come full circle as you encounter yet another group. This happens to be that group of persons you probably once thought could not possibly be found in the American society. It is the very different group of persons whose style remains unique and exceedingly remarkable. At times, it seems that they were born different. But this is America. No one is born different. And since they are Americans, they are also supposedly equal.

In this rather special group are those people who demonstrate a markedly different approach to life's issues than the others. Here, it appears the approach is to let things go their way while the victims see nothing, appreciate nothing, and worry about nothing. These persons are often forced by factors beyond their grasp to amble around as their spirits resign to fate. This instance of fatalism isn't exactly a course consciously chosen by them but a situation blessed upon them by an incidence of nature that effectively makes them nonparticipants in the planning of their lives and essentially absent in the critical circumstances that shape their fortune.

In essence, these persons are nonactors in their own lives, which seem to let their problems dictate the course of every activity around them. They seem to depend upon the play of time, which might effect a change of circumstances with no predetermined outcome. And as it often happens, this passage of time plays out an outcome with a very unnurturing touch. At this point, these persons proceed totally mindlessly in abject despondence. Their forms drift out of concert with the being, wearing a look of pity and disconcerted presence. They can hardly interact with others, and their actions only mimic a semblance of warped reality. In substance, they only go through the motions, essentially operating with a set of transient nuances of realism. As their situation degenerates, their instinctive reactions to life appear to dance to a very different tune as they gradually drift away from everyone else. In time, these persons drop out of reach as their beings further degenerate into one of vacancy immediately announced by a presence of aloof impersonality.

They begin to amble around visibly absentmindedly, their gait fragmented by the burden of mental dislocation.

But these folks too hustle. For it is still America, and hustling is a lifelong occupation, irrespective of your mental disposition. You may encounter these persons in the midst of their perambulation and witness their feet uncoordinatedly hurried and sashaying in irreversibly discordant steps. They often alter their movement as they stop and gaze into the distance, their eyes, however, betraying the mindlessness of a stare into nothingness. These steps lead them to nowhere readily accessible to others. It is their journey. It is their trip. It is their walk that invariably finds them waltzing out of the scene. They ultimately find an abode or an abode finds them essentially dwelling permanently on the outskirts of life and dealing from the periphery of existence.

They are often referred to as the insane.

"The insane," the traveler ruminates. He lets his mind drift a bit, a seeming structured drift in search of something definitive about the human mind and its inherent fragility. He wonders why the fragility but remains rather inclined to shy away from exploring the possibility of a perfect mind, perfect in the sense of encapsulating the unique circumstance of being both infallible and immortal; a mind simply without blemish and beyond the constraints of vulnerability.

He lets his thoughts play themselves out as he focuses on the possibility that, no doubt, some unfortunately insane people existed in your old society and perhaps were shunned by the society as it happens here. But perhaps there is a difference in the way your new society treats this group. In your old society, these persons are rarely banished from the community or ostracized and quarantined. They are considered members of the community who were dealt an unfortunate hand by nature. And, by the way, interaction with the insane has never been known to afflict others with whatever ails the broken minds.

In that society, as in many others outside America, there is an understanding among the citizens that creates an atmosphere that accommodates and accepts these persons as members of the community. This aspect of other cultures appears to make their systems more human oriented and tends to present the societies as a community of humanity for the sake and welfare of humanity.

And incidentally, the very presence of the insane plays a critical role of reminding humankind of the transiency of its existence and the inherent fragility of its mind.

Whatever role you play in this society, you are part of the community and a contributor to that which is truly great and a subscriber to that which is not exactly the most appealing. As a member of the community, you may watch with concern the treatment and handling of the insane, or you could simply focus on yourself and your own and let things play out as they may as long as you are not directly affected by the socially sanctioned activities in your community.

There is something, however, about being human, and this could be the ability to be touched by societal incidents that treat the powerless with a heavy hand and purely mechanical and robotic approach to their plight. You most likely would be touched by some of the treatments handed down to these insane persons. As you watch them, you are immediately aware that their minds have changed. Their posture has been altered by a different set of realities and their presence diminished and virtually absent as their being responds to the vacancy in their eyes.

You may be moved, perhaps by a touch of pity, as you witness them being corralled into dwellings of confinement and their movements restricted according to the dictates of prescribed regimentation. It is possible that, like some people in your adopted American community, you've learned a way of seeing these treatments but letting your mind override the sense of pity and focusing on whatever be your business, thus taking a stand of neutral disposition. In essence, you'd have chosen to let things be the way they are, thus preferring pretentious inaction to a very definite stand of personal involvement.

On the other hand, you may seek to raise your voice or yell through the very effective silence of informed protest and speak against this practice.

You soon learn that in your newly adopted American community, nothing changes of its own accord, particularly for the better. This is a culture that gloats about its uniqueness and flaunts its abundance, but it attempts to let you know that despite this element of uniqueness, which boasts the capability to raise every one of its citizens from the misery of poverty and despair to the height of basic and comfortable sufficiency, the society essentially owes you nothing. It is within your capability, it is assumed, to assimilate. It is within your capability to improve your lot, and all these possibilities lie within the parameters of your choices.

These assurances, which constitute the fundamental basis of a social contract, are stated with the understanding that, as a member of the community, you are duty bound to contribute toward the betterment of the society. It is expected that the individual has the capacity to grasp that, in substance, the society is not exactly an intangible element. He, as well as his neighbors, are the society, and their presence is the actualization of the society.

This statement by the system becomes an affirmation of the societal belief in the capabilities and the importance of the individual. The rather implicit message belying this belief is that, in order for the society to thrive, it is necessary that every individual aims to make a contribution toward the betterment of the society.

The message is there for the individual to grasp that, in essence, the society is not exactly an instance of pure abstraction.

This message, in the American society, goes farther than in most other places because it encourages the individual to have respect for the rights of others, including the appreciation of their privacy. It is expected that, through the same process, the individual not only respects and appreciates his neighbor's personhood but also recognizes and accepts his inalienable right to existence.

Such a pragmatic approach to life in the American system seems quite noble, people oriented, and pretty advanced. But the apparent goodness of the approach is undermined by some of the socially sanctioned methods of dealing with the less fortunate segments of the society. It is remarkable, however, that, in spite of the shortcomings in the culture, which its detractors see as its paramount fault of being plastic and sterile, the emphasis on the individual's right to existence stands as exceptionally unique and admirable. But, as the detractors claim, this feature of the culture is ultimately diminished by the emphasis on individuality and the absolute need for the accumulation of wealth. Such diminishment in the system, it is believed, is further worsened by the fact that the less fortunate in the society are often blamed for whatever misfortune has befallen them.

As a satisfied transplant who is pleased with his acquisitions and impressed by the prospects and promise of gaining more, you may find fault with this line of thinking by the detractors of the culture. On the other hand, it is possible that despite the level of your success in the American society you could find ample evidence in the system that lends credence to the views of the detractors.

Perhaps in your old culture, as in most non-Western cultures, the life of the individual is regarded as precious. Some cultures even appear to endow a person's life with a certain measure of sanctity. In these other cultures, such person-oriented features are often played out loudly and visibly. And in the process of living according to the precepts of these features of the culture, the neighbors preach their benefits and the children sing the attributes often in folkloric renditions of appreciation for the exceptional quality of their cultural tenets.

These aspects of your old culture appear to elevate it and make it more accommodating and nurturing. But depending on where and which culture you came from, what you find in America may be the only perfect system there is for you. This could be the very best, if you hail from one of those societies in which respect for your neighbor's life is preached but not practiced. In these societies, respect for the neighbor is not mutual and mutuality of respect is often determined by who is interacting with whom. The elite and the privileged demand and get respect often at the expense of the less fortunate members of the society.

In some of those societies in which respect for the individual is truly practiced as part of the social norm, the individual's life is not only respected but also viewed as very unique. And this aspect of the culture gives the social system a uniqueness that is close to inviolability.

But in your new pluralistic American society, which is home to all kinds from every known culture on the planet, such views regarding the culture are frowned upon. It is bourgeois, some would say. It is elitist, others would claim. And yet, others would go so far as to insist it is racist in its practical application and essentially divisive in its intentions. But you find they all agree there is no substituent element for its social benefits. And that's another area in which the American culture stands out.

Now you are inclined to wonder what the hell is going on in this, your newly adopted American culture.

You may be quite lucky, at this point of your stay, to have learned how not to question most of the practices and norms that you notice in the society. You take what you see and work with it as best you can, for there are just too many incidents in the system that would further confuse you if you decided to seek the whys and hows, which give rise to their occurrence.

You live with the system as it plays out in accord with the social preferences instituted as norms.

You may be inclined to pause a moment, however, to find your bearing as you witness some aspects of the system that seem somewhat beyond interesting. You learn that, as you proceed to join the mad rush for the acquisition of toys, everyone around you hustles just the same, including those who have lost their minds and those who have lost their lives. And as you'll realize, this happens to be a cultural phenomenon that the folks refuse to lose. You hear the neighbors who inform you that this cultural habit is only a necessary part of the game of life as everyone plays toward the same goal. Then, you witness as the dead, at his funeral, is loaded with toys as his loved ones throw a few items of material goods into his grave. It is as if those he is leaving behind want to avoid an instance of social embarrassment by making sure the poor fellow is not laying there empty-handed.

You can imagine the topic of the neighborhood gossip, if this fellow is lying in his grave fitted out in his old pants and nothing thrown in to extol the family's image. God help us all!

CHAPTER II

A Changing Person

D ID YOU LOSE your sense of humor when you arrived in America, or did you lose your sense of pity and the capacity for empathy? Perhaps a few things that might have shocked you in the past are beginning to be accepted as necessary occurrences or incidents that are simply unavoidable in the daily preoccupations of humankind; you wonder what's happening to that person who in the not-so-distant past empathized with the plight of every unfortunate soul. Depending on your inclinations, you'd distinguish one kind of person from the other, and you'd find reason to exculpate some persons in their transgressions. You did this because you felt that some people have been raised to believe in doing such things while some are raised in a more socially acceptable way. And because you wore the emblem of humanity on your person, you often found room for forgiveness, though you may not exactly be willing to readily turn the other cheek.

In your current experiences here in America, this mind-set is beginning to change; and rather strangely, you find yourself becoming comfortable with this change. You dare to wonder why, but this is short-lived, for you are rather quick to see this as an adaptive inclination begun in the process of assimilation. This change is also comfortably falling into place since for you, it has become a process of gaining something and losing another. As a transplant, you occasionally wonder, however, if what you are gaining is worth more than you are losing. You wonder if, in the end, any beneficial cultural traits, particularly those ones that have served you so well in the past, are worth losing. Perhaps quite in keeping with your expectations, it is an inevitable process, one that ushers in new prospects and a synthesis of events, albeit disparate and in opposition to the others. But as long as the end results of these changes serve useful purposes, your decision seems quite sound, and such soundness validates the utility therein.

You are beginning to find that it is not simply your bodily presence that is going through changes but your mind as well. You realize it is your mental state, most importantly, that is changing. But it would seem that as long as the change in mental state is well accommodated, as long as it is worn and utilized in a proper manner, you can rest comfortably with the change. On occasions, this change may seem very profound, and this sets you thinking about yourself. You wonder about what motivates you, you wonder how malleable your mind is, and you wonder how much in control of your mind you really are. You can't help but admit to yourself that your newly adopted American culture is having a profound effect on you because, in what might seem like honest comparisons to your previous self, you find various reasons to criticize your old self.

As a person raised in a different culture, you may find yourself engaging in such mental exercises pretty often and you may even find it comforting. And in times of adversity, such predilections become unavoidable preoccupations, which help by keeping you focused because in such times, your newly adopted American culture has a rather interesting way of reminding you that you are pretty much on your own. Such periods of adversity also remind you that in your new culture, perhaps as distinct from the old, the subject of persons can take on a rather impersonal element. You've heard it said that there is something in the American system that is suggestive of the dispensability of the human being. The word is that this aspect of the culture is not exactly preached or taught in any manner but that the culture appears to encourage it in its practical application. Now you are somewhat suspicious of some of the tidings of your new culture. But perhaps as a measure of comfort, you are quick to question the validity of such suspicions. You might even find yourself dismissing such thoughts as errant misconceptions that drift into the mind of their own accord.

Perhaps you've held the belief all along that the person of the individual is endowed with attributes that guarantee the uniqueness and the indispensability of the being. And your previous culture probably encouraged you to view yourself this way and, by extension, others around you.

But you get the feeling that the emphasis in your new society is different. The initial impressions you are getting in your new culture is that of a culture suffused with the trappings of technology and adorned with orderly arrangements of both the animate and the inanimate. You notice buildings including other structures placed in preplanned arrangements that supposedly enhance their utility and functionality. Their uniqueness is evidenced by their ability to structure the movements of the folks within and, at times, limit the temptation of a careless fellow who might otherwise entertain the idea of wandering through the wrong place. These structures serve useful purposes, nonetheless.

You probably also notice that you could get fined a sizable amount for littering while the penalty for what may seem like a more serious misdeed could fetch a lesser punishment. But you are beginning to see the reasoning behind such concepts. It costs more to clean and tidy up the community than it takes to rectify the misbehavior of a recalcitrant fellow who chooses to disrupt his neighbor's peace of mind or violate his personal space. You like and appreciate the efficiency of the systems. Communication isn't just easy and working fine. It is almost miraculous in its instant functionality. The roads are quite well maintained, and there is added comfort as you notice the sign that assures you that it is your *tax dollars at work*. Really?

It is not just the fact that the roads and the structures work so well, and it is not exactly the fact that they work that arrests your imagination but the coordination and the apparent simplicity inherent in their mechanics that encourages your sense of appreciation. As you witness the whole system work with the folks in an interactive manner, you can't help but feel the touch of mixed emotions. You feel both impressed and somewhat dismayed, particularly at the thought that all you are witnessing requires money for their use and this is one very, very necessary item you must have in order to enjoy the workings of most of these objects.

Now you are beginning to sense the inherent discomfort of disappointment. But it's all right, and you are comfortable with the feeling because you've heard it said that money is the sole guarantor of the emancipation and participation in the American society. You also wonder at the frequency with which the various things sold at the stores appear to change form. The most striking example of this is the sudden change in items on store shelves as they seem to go through

IKE C. UDEH

rapid transformation right before your eyes. You bought an item from a store the day before. Then you noticed the very next day that the same item is now marked *new and improved*. You then noticed that the price went up, but the content was less than when you first bought it. Now your excitement at the rate at which things get improved so fast and so impressively is short-lived, but it's all right. This feeling of disappointment is soon gone because, as a member of the culture, you can readily accept such changes. You can accept the possibility that it's not just the content of the item that is improved. The system of measurement as well is now improved—often to give you less for more money.

As a transplant, you are loving it all, however, because not only are you still here in America, but you've also changed your status— an emphatic affirmation of the tenets of this culture. Through the process of your willing participation and the drive to assimilate, you become part of the culture like everyone else. Some transplants like you begin to take on some of the unique behaviors as soon as they begin to feel a sense of belonging. They join the residents in their habit of asking every suspected new arrival, "You speak with an accent. Where did you come from?" In some cases, the questioner, who often puts on an air of pseudo surprise and excitement, holds back the statement actually playing in his mind, "Looks like you just got off the boat."

Some transplants even find it necessary to affirm their status as a bona fide American, far removed from the mannerisms of the newer arrivals by adopting some of these behaviors, and they don't hesitate to tell the newly arrived how to behave themselves. Some are even quick to instruct others to love it or leave it. If you happen to witness this remarkable interaction, you might notice that the recipient of this instruction looks somewhat sheepish, with a mixed gaze of masked disdain and envy. But then, you feel it's none of your business and rest with the thought that it's all part of tradition. A part of you, however, may wonder whatever happened to your sense of understanding. But in the end, you find a way to live with it. And as you seek to explain for your own peace of mind the slight but noticeable difference in the comportment of the new arrival, you might even find your thoughts whispering to you, "Must have just got off the boat."

In American society, the individual, particularly the transplant, is always conscious of the fact that it is necessary for his own well-being to assimilate. And the process takes various forms, one of them being mimicking some of the behaviors of the resident folks. Often, the manner in which the copied behavior is displayed may not seem mimetic because the mimicker plays it so well that it fits perfectly with the norm.

Some of the transplants, particularly those who have found a way to Americanize without appearing to work too hard to fit in, manage to assimilate into the society faster than others. They, at times, even appear to be more American than the residents. But as a transplant, as you assimilate, however, your perceptions change. Your person, as well, goes through changes. It is even believed that your being is recreated. It is a process of near total transformation. In the process of assimilation, people go through various experiences, some of which can directly affect their faith. As a transplant, you could find the avenue to assimilation through religion, and depending on what religious tenets shaped your faith in the old culture, the recreation of your being in the process of assimilation could be effected through the sanctity of extra-ardent religiosity. In this case, your being attains the added endowment of preternatural emancipation. And this process often happens when, as a transplant, your very first intimate encounter is with a resident who happens to be loaded with the Book. As you assimilate through this process, you eventually become, in concrete terms, the tangible manifestation of successful homiletics. It is said, more often by those subscribers to the benefits of this process of assimilation, that the individual's assimilation happens much easier and smoother.

Apparently, there are no rough edges in the assimilation of those transplants who experience this process. And soon enough, these individuals find the church, or as it happens more often, the church finds them. Some even join the resident folks—in this instance, the brethren—as they mount the podium to preach the Word. And this is quite OK, for these assimilated persons are said to have chosen the path to assimilation through the Word.

You may be lucky if you encounter these persons, including their resident escort, in your neighborhood. They are quick to smile while putting on an air of the humble servant coming to you with a friendly, welcome-to-the-Word demeanor. They try to address you with the utmost respect, beneath which you notice a slight tinge of poorly masked impatience. They are quick to hurry off if there is something about your presence suggesting a difficult prospect with nothing tangible for

IKE C. UDEH

conversion. And they often make a point of leaving you with a word or two about the significance of their mission and the benefits of the Word. As they depart, you suspect there is something sacred about their gait and wonder if you'd just missed a rare opportunity for redemption.

Some people will tell you that the process of assimilation rides on your mind-set, which is determined by priorities. They point to others who are said to assimilate through a different process based on the implicit belief in materialism. For those people who choose this process, material acquisition becomes a goal of such paramount importance that everything else flows from this undertaking. To those people who subscribe to the process of the Word, these persons for whom materialism is a cherished preference are said to have missed the way. In keeping with the American culture, however, this latter group is often seen as the wealthy and successful. They are classified as the social elite and, consequently, the privileged. They are often criticized but, nonetheless, envied.

And, yes, there is envy among the others as they wish for everything this privileged set can display. They want the riches. They desire the comfort provided by these riches. But they seek to comfort themselves with the belief that their own wealth and privilege lie somewhere beyond here. Of course, there is consolation in knowing that the privilege and wealth, which lie beyond your reach, await you somewhere beyond here; and this consolation is further blessed with the belief that these goods are guaranteed in their superabundance. And, no, there is no dichotomy here. It is very American and perfectly OK to expect a privileged and wealthy situation in your hereafter. After all, if you fail to attain riches here, you can mitigate your disappointment by comfortably placing your luck in the firmaments. And let's face it, you are talking the firmaments—and that's precisely where you have the guts to tell your previously wealthy neighbor to go to hell. You see, the firmaments have a funny way of protecting you from the machinations of the previously wealthy. So as some will tell you, this adds another touch of glory to the trappings of your new society. Just because you failed to acquire all the toys you wanted does not necessarily make you a total loser. For as long as you truly believe, you'll be very OK when you pass.

The more assimilated you become in America, the fewer contradictions you see in some of these aspects of your new culture because you begin to subscribe to the belief that these social concepts sustain hope in their practical application and, through the inherence of their subsumed implications, provide the citizens with the capacity for surviving in abject destitution. You realize this system of guaranteeing wealth in the hereafter also provides the very necessary benefit of social order within the society.

You cannot condemn this practice, because something about your person makes you want to belong to the lucky group. Of course, it is rather difficult not to feel this way because the possibility of great material acquisition is about the most important factor which motivated your move in the first place. So, you notice this aspect of class in your newly adopted classless society; but you are aware of the varying situations of the two groups. Then you weigh the consequences of belonging to the rather unfortunate group and, of course, you strive for the lucky camp. And, yes, there is something about getting your wealth in the firmaments that doesn't sit very well. At this point, you are well motivated to hustle harder. You dream of striking it rich. You wish there's a place you can find wealth as you take the next exit. You strive to keep up the pace and hope that your being has not been endowed with the misfortune of having your own wealth placed in the firmaments. And, no, you dare not give up hope, for this is a lifelong occupation. You sharpen your skills at every turn and seek to improve your style daily; and, at the end of the day, you count your dimes and whisper to yourself, "Damn it, I'm gonna make it!"

It has all been designed to work this way in your newly adopted American culture. Everything is designed to fit into a preplanned process; and the process, in turn, is structured to sustain everything, including the people within. As for you, you are finally beginning to fit in quite well. You are even surprised at the ease with which you accept some of the aspects of the culture that you would have found abhorring in the past. But you are comfortable with this rather instant switch of perspectives because the move to a different place, by its very nature, implies the willingness not only to relocate but also to adapt to the new environment and live with both its merits and demerits. And since the reality of your new environment, like the previous one, is manifested in its culture and social mores, your decision to move also implied a yearning for change, which in itself encourages an open mind ready and willing to try something new and possibly different.

As your perspectives change, there is often the added fun of trying sometimes very hard to remain who you were when you first arrived. For some, this activity takes on the form of emphasizing the differences in pronunciation. They speak English all right, but apparently, they wallow in the heavily accented pronunciation of every word. Besides the possible difficulty in picking up the local accent, you suspect there is something else gained from this practice, the most likely ones being difference, shock, novelty, and the perceived element of exoticism. And, yes, this behavior too is included in the process of assimilation.

CHAPTER III

The Way It Was

A S YOUR ASSIMILATION progresses, the novelty in practically everything around you diminishes. You are at about the point at which the need for success is beginning to outweigh everything else. This change in perspective does not happen by incident but for the incidence—that being the inclination for success. Your needs begin to change. They become increasingly more complicated and thus more difficult to meet. But something about your sense of caution reminds you that you are, in the end, more comfortable with defining your needs in simple terms and in line with your capabilities. This rather basic sense of caution also helps you negotiate the more difficult aspects of the American culture, which for a new arrival could pose some problems. But you are aware of the fact that in time, you've begun to work with a set of changed perspectives on life and, consequently, a differently defined set of needs. It is a different culture in a very different society. There are various situational differences between the American and your previous society, which may necessitate drastic changes in everything from clothing to diet; and the change in diet, particularly, could be very significant. There is also a difference in expectations, both social and personal.

In your newly adopted American culture, you are constantly reminded of your right to food, comfort, and shelter.

Most essentially, you are reminded of your inalienable right to existence. With such rights, which are often explicitly stated, you find that your expectations change because now, perhaps unlike your previous culture, these basic rights embolden your self-perception. You begin to see your person as a truly dignified component of humanity.

Perhaps in your old society these rights were spoken about, or even taught, but rarely enforced or encouraged. They probably were legislated and mandated by law but were often reserved for the few who have the power or resources to demand and get them. So here is a very striking example of differences in cultures, which not only awaken a certain sense of self-appreciation but also incentivize your drive for success. Incidentally, this becomes an important aspect of your new culture, which not only affirms your decision to move but also encourages a fresh look at your capabilities as an individual.

If there was any latent sense of diffidence in your being, a fresh look at your capabilities provides a tool that helps to overcome this feeling. There is also a feeling of vindication that seeks to nullify any traces of guilt perhaps associated with the decision to move to a different culture. To most, this becomes an aspect of the new culture demonstrably uplifting to the individual and incalculably authenticating to the self, particularly in those critical moments when self-confidence becomes a very necessary instrument for survival.

Along with these very admirable cultural tenets come some aspects that not only tend to undermine your enthusiasm but also raise some questions as to the propriety of assimilation into your new culture. Perhaps an example of this is when the need for self-authentication becomes the dominant element in person-to-person interactions. But you have to assimilate because you need to. After all, assimilation remains the primary process of fitting in. And so, as you weigh some aspects of the culture, which may not exactly be very appealing to you, you analyze your approach to that which is great and that which is not the most elegant. You seek to find a proper approach to what could potentially become a dilemma. Your goal is to ultimately find effective ways to negotiate through the maze of the American system and find a proper process that allows your assimilation to proceed with fewer distractions.

Your attempt to overcome your doubts with regard to your assimilation, however, can be further discouraged by some of the various things you notice around you. You notice that some of the practices in your new culture are similar to what you were used to back home but you are finding that the only noticeable difference is in their application. Of course, people moved around and did what they wanted in your old culture. They also had dreams and felt free to aspire toward those dreams. But often those dreams came with limitations inherent in the scarcity of resources, and this often meant the dreams were not realizable or only partially so. But in the American culture, you appreciate the fact that not only can you have dreams but the culture itself encourages you to dream, with the implied assurance that your dreams are realizable. It also becomes more encouraging to dream if you are reminded that, if you toil at it, you'll realize it.

This aspect of the American culture makes it more appealing and definitely more attractive, and it is one of the preeminent factors that make a lot of people in other cultures want to immigrate to America. But as you begin to explore the various possibilities in this society, you also notice the constant hunger and sustained drive for change. It is as if nothing is designed or expected to last past the limits of its appeal; and the shelf life of this appeal is often determined by the attendant novelty, which is inherently transient.

Like everyone else around you, particularly the tradition-oriented residents, you wonder if anything really endures in this society. You might entertain some fear that, at this rate of change, including the society's ever-increasing need for change, even those very worthy aspects of the culture may not endure.

As you listen to some of the residents who may feel the way you do, you hope that any changes in the cultural trends will only be transient. Perhaps your hope could be grounded on the possibility that the exemplary aspects of the culture are firmly basic. They are fundamental in defining both the people within the culture and the hopes and aspirations that sustain them. Some of those residents with eyes on tradition often claim that such sustaining elements of the culture ride on principles that lend vitality to the people's views on life and their perspectives on the human course. As a transplant, you may be inclined to accept this view since it provides a measure of reassurance that the culture has essential tools that tend to resist radical changes.

Thus, you are left with the feeling that the American culture, particularly the very fundamental aspects of it, are properly resilient; and you begin to suspect that this factor of resiliency enables the culture to withstand the impact of transient changes, which ultimately play themselves out as mere instances of generational predilections.

As you further explore the American culture and its strength, you appreciate more the central factor underlying the strength and the vitality of the culture. Everything that you suspect defines the culture and the people rides on freedom. This aspect of the culture is so central to the essence of life in the American society that it narrates the past, it defines the present, and it projects the future. It explicitly guarantees the right to existence and implicitly proclaims the vitality of the society as an absolutely independent nation.

In essence, freedom in this society becomes an indispensable element for the vitality of authentic human existence.

The more reassured you are about your new society, the more you are inclined to speed up your drive for success. You proceed with the action of carving out your own niche while staying focused on whatever be your occupation. And, of course, along with this, you hustle, like everyone else around you, to beef up your collection of toys.

This appears to make it rather comforting to note that the American culture in the end will remain basically the same and not lose those qualities you admired in the first place. But then you notice some changes, particularly within the social structure. Your fears are not exactly assuaged but very likely rendered subtle and easy to live with. Your belief in the substance of the culture is further strengthened by your resolve and the knowledge that you are now beginning to carve out your own niche. And as this knowledge plays within your thoughts, you invariably notice the touch of self-reassessment. You seek to analyze your reactions and the manner in which you respond to things that directly affect your person. You may find surprise in your reactions to some of these responses, for they may be very different than they would have been in the past. You wonder if assimilation means an absolute change in perspectives. You certainly would rather see your assimilation proceed in a thoughtful manner, thus allowing adequate room for analysis and logical progression from one human system to another. You realize, however, that the process of assimilation often happens instinctively and somewhat subconsciously. You don't exactly sit down to think or plan assimilation. It often happens as you seek to belong and participate.

Now your self-reassessment takes on a more in-depth format. This shouldn't consume you, however; or it could become an unnecessary preoccupation, which slows the pace and limits the prospects of timely participation in the system. So you find a comfortable explanation for the exercise. You may settle with the thought that it was only a minor distraction, unavoidable and necessitated by nostalgia. It was essentially a subterfusion designed to keep you from straying too far too fast.

But you are aware that these moments of self-reassessment will occur again. You decide to analyze any issue as it arises. You size it up and compartmentalize the various aspects into meaningful clusters of logical preferences. You decide on a sequential order that lies in concordance with your order of preferences. Ultimately, you ameliorate your discomfort by rendering yourself capable of dealing with most difficult cultural issues by analyzing them and defining them according to their utility. As you become more comfortable with this format, you feel there is an answer for every issue, particularly those that directly impact your decisions and perspectives in America.

You may experience such mental preoccupations so frequently as to make you wonder if you are on the right track to proper assimilation. You may also wonder if you should strive to retain most of your previous perspectives on life. But you are quick to reject such thoughts because you can find reasons to do just that. And, of course, there is an abundance of reasons, the most salient one being that so far you've found no reason for a return to your previous culture. There is also the fact that you've come to see the necessity in striving to acquire as many toys as possible, precisely as encouraged in your new culture. You proceed with the action of carving out your own niche and staying focused on whatever be your business.

Occasionally, you may get sidetracked by your neighbor, who appears to be moving forward in leaps and bounds and with what appears to be extraordinary success. Or perhaps you notice he has a system that seems to go totally against yours and that of others around you despite the appearance of the absence of reason in his method. But you suspect that this may be his preferred way of living his life. At this point, you feel you'd be better served if you minded your own business, for you've learned the rather simple anecdote that, in America, all kicking of the ball is toward the goal.

In time, there is growth in your person and you notice this in some of the ways and manners in which you respond to the various incidents that impact your daily life. Obviously, your perspectives on things are changing; and you, as a person, are going through changes that may not all be easy to accommodate. This could be particularly true in those moments when you find yourself dealing with questions or doubts with regard to some of the things you previously held as credos. In such a case, a change in perspective could be not exactly the best process. But since you've come to accept the fact that your primary objective in America, like many around you, is to achieve your goals, you feel it is only necessary that any change in perspective serves a useful purpose. You are comfortable with this view because it is of paramount importance that, as a transplant living in America, you strive to achieve your goals. This is one aspect of the culture you learned immediately upon arrival, and practically all that is going on around you speaks to this. It is also becoming a personal expectation.

Not only do you entertain this as a personal expectation, but you also realize that it underlies that aspect of the American culture that emphasizes that you should fend for yourself. The corollary to this becomes self-sufficiency. And as you begin to break it down to its basics, you find that this aspect of the culture plays in concert with that preeminent American cultural tenet: freedom. And oh yes, everything that defines your new culture—everything that sustains the swagger, the spirit of individuality and the can-do attitude—is firmly anchored on this principle of freedom.

Invariably, you also find that your occasional feelings of doubt have little drive to sustain them. They may be necessary but nevertheless brief. You even wonder, at times, how transient these moments of doubt are. You are surprised at how quickly they come and go. You are comfortable with this, however, for something tells you that the manner in which these doubts and questions come and go is part of a learning experience in America. You've come to learn the necessity, including the benefits, of fending for yourself. Your concern now becomes the need to make sure that the end of your endeavor justifies the means as long as it does not obviate the stipulated principles of socially acceptable practice.

And like most people in your newly adopted American society, as you resurface from your mental preoccupations, you seek to refocus your attention on the business at hand. But it is clear to you that, as you go about your daily business, your thoughts cover various aspects of the goings-on around you. Perhaps you are beginning to see some of the fruits of your labor, albeit small, but appreciable nonetheless. You may not find the moment to gloat or briefly wallow in the appreciation of your small success, for there is something about the culture that reminds you that, in America, everything passes rather quickly; it is all brief, and all you've acquired is subject to being lost at any point. But you still aspire to build up your nest and acquire as many toys as you can. Perhaps you may wonder what it is all about, but the system nudges you on. It is designed to work this way, which may make you wonder sometimes if there is really room for negotiation.

At this point, you may be analyzing and considering the meaning and place of the individual within the two cultures, the American and your previous culture. You suspect that this aspect of both cultures, which deals with the place of the individual in the society, plays very differently here than in your previous culture. You look at the differences, and you feel they are rather striking. But you feel that both aspects have their benefits, and these are often realized in the spirit of their practical application. You feel that this aspect of the American culture that immediately concerns the individual lacks the touch of humanity when considered in the abstract. But your inquiry may enable you to see that in its application, there is something realized in accord with the intended benefit and this perception may improve your initial impression.

In your old culture, there was an emphasis on the community as a whole. There was an extension from the family to the neighbor and from that to the community and on to the world at large. It is a progression that utilizes the person to define the essence of the community. The individual was and remains a very essential part of the family, and this process tends to de-emphasize the factor of individuality. There is, in this process, the added benefit of mental gratification, which further encourages a sense of not being alone. And this becomes a necessary tool that sustains the person in his misfortunes and adversities. It is a great feeling to know that you are not alone in your adversities.

And, yes, there are some negatives in your previous system. In that culture, you find that most of your life decisions are either made for you or you can make and realize them only with the blessings of others. You also find that your business is everyone's business. In some of its more intense applications, the individual could be ostracized and at times rusticated for what has been deemed a serious transgression by others or by someone in the community. In some of these instances, there may be no proof or convincing evidence required. It all could have been motivated by the guilty individual's penchant for preferring to be a loner and always wanting to go it alone, especially in matters that are not so commonplace among the community. In some instances, such actions of ostracism could be irreversible. One of the failing aspects in this system made more obvious, not necessarily by its detractors but by its immediately obvious lack of due process, is that of systemic opportunism. You could get nailed by one who does not particularly like your presence. Your plight is made even worse if your accuser happens to be among the interlocutors in an interlocutory system that often bars you from speaking. You are only present to hear what has been decided to be your fate. It is often stated, more by the system's detractors, that this process could also retard the individual's progress. According to some, this is especially true because the de-emphasis on individuality has the inherent element of blunting a more daring perspective on life.

In your newly adopted American culture, you suspect the reverse is true. You are encouraged right from infancy to learn and develop the knack for managing yourself and your affairs by yourself within your own boundaries. This, in turn, begins to lay the foundation for self-sufficiency. You are, at this point of infancy, toying with the foundations of personal strength of character and the substrates of individualism. Along with this comes a good measure of self-confidence—the fundamental fabric of a can-do attitude. There is also a daring outlook on life that comes with this system. In this system, it is presumed that the individual is more achieving. Or is he really?

And, of course, there are some negatives in this system. According to some of its detractors, the more individualistic you are, the more alone you find your confines. The more alone within the parameters of your confines of life, the more you have to go it alone, even in the face of adversity. You are dealing with life and its vicissitudes, which guarantee various periods of adversity. When adversity strikes, as it most certainly will, you are inclined to want to go it alone lest you be considered a failure or simply lacking the tools for survival in difficult times. And if your predicament should demand external help for your survival, your failure could prove your undoing.

In some of its more unfortunate implications, this aspect of your new culture, it is often believed, becomes disconcertingly empty, depressingly impersonal, and profoundly lacking humanity. You become a system unto yourself. But you might find some of the proponents of this aspect of the culture touting what they perceive as an existentialist quality to it. This quality, the proponents of the culture claim, becomes one of its more salient elements of attraction and also lends credence to one of the culture's overriding principles of the individual's absolute belief in his own confidence and capacities. This aspect of the culture has the appearance of rendering it supremely sufficient for negotiating through life and its abundant intricacies.

This is one of the more vulnerable aspects of the American culture according to its detractors. It is believed that this aspect of the culture has a rather seductive nature that tends to negate any reason for the belief in any force, instance, or occasion beyond the human sphere. After all, the belief in the perceived fact that you are sufficient unto yourself, particularly if you strike it right, lends credence to your choices and becomes an affirmation of your existentialist approach to life. Stretched to its fullest potential, as perceived by its detractors, existentialism, coupled with material success, becomes essentially irresistible as it dangles the attractiveness of wealth in your thoughts and effectively negates any rudiments of a logical drive for balance that unites the tangible life and the spiritual.

But now you are in America. The emphasis is definitely on the individual. Materialism is either loudly preached or implicitly emphasized. You witness the trappings of plenty and wealth all around you. You experience the unquestionable comfort provided by the good things around, all mostly the results of individual dreams, individual effort, and a daring approach to life. But you are also questioning and seeking answers beyond the obvious, and this exercise is further egged on by the fact that the culture encourages inquiry and promotes an investigative look into every topic or instance. Even the very process of experiencing and living according to the dictates of the culture encourages analysis and reexamination of that which may be considered unequivocal or absolute.

There is a chance that you may find yourself at a crossroads as you follow your process of inquiry. In your previous culture, humanity was emphasized; and this, its proponents claim, often creates an atmosphere that encourages a belief in the existence of some force or being, perhaps uncreated but supremely sufficient, to firmly anchor their aspirations and, ultimately, the very essence of their being. In that culture, the people claim, there is ample room for them to realize their dreams and, at the same time, look up to something beyond them as a process of affirmation of their being. They often entertain the belief that with

IKE C. UDEH

a strong belief in the existence of a force beyond the present, a force that provides something beyond the capabilities of humankind, their existence is superior to that which is devoid of such concepts. This concept is said to work for its proponents.

As you ponder these opposing statements, which posit contrasting claims of the two different cultures, you may find yourself in a quandary. You may choose to save yourself the mental anguish by simply foregoing such thoughts and concentrating your energy on whatever business is at hand. You may, on the other hand, choose to wallow in them, thereby preferring a preoccupation of intense mental exercise as an appropriate item for momentary escapism. There could be a fleeting sensation of instant mental gratification here because you are not exactly searching for adequate answers, or looking for resolution. You are only entertaining these thoughts and toying with what has a semblance of satisfaction. You did not shy away from them, and this creates the impression of a conscious engagement of that which appears to lie beyond the reach of immediate resolution.

If you engage in such mental exercises often enough, you may find an unexpected but gratifying benefit of appearing too busy and focused on your thoughts to participate in any debates on personal and social issues. This is the look you put on when you don't really feel like participating in a process of an intense debate that detracts from your immediate concerns. In such moments, you worry only about those things that have immediate impact on your life. As for the distinctions in cultural perspectives, between the American and your previous culture, you let time and your experience in America provide the answers.

A part of the picture is clear, however, as it probably was back in your old culture. The end game is always the same, irrespective of where you are. Perhaps an unexpected benefit of your mental exercise is that it brings you full circle, right back to the prospects of meeting your needs both immediate and for the future. You proceed to examine your responsibilities, both to yourself and to your newly adopted community. You count your gains and size up the losses, and this could often become the primary determinant in deciding where to go next and how to proceed. But this may not present any problems for you because knowing the American culture and its emphasis on every man on his own, your reliance on yourself and your capacities will often keep you on track. This self-reliance also helps you stay in step with everyone else. As it is, you must, in your new culture, always know how and when to find your cue, strap on your boots, and march along. This process always finds you quite prepared to take it all in stride. And as you proceed, you remind yourself—or something reminds you as it often happens in America—that, in this game of life, everyone plays for himself and God plays for all. And oh yes, this system always reminds you with a constant whisper. Every man for himself and God for us all.

As a transplant, perhaps you are beginning to feel somewhat comfortable with your place in the community, but you are not feeling very satisfied with whatever material gains you've made. However, you feel you are making a headway and gradually moving up whatever ladder you've set up for yourself; and something tells you to stick to your plans. You may not know exactly how your plans will work out, and you may not know precisely what will be the end result of your endeavors, but you stick to your plans anyway and try to stay on course, for you know only too well that you lose your track if you lose sight of your goals.

At times, however, despite your best efforts to stay focused, you find yourself wavering and entertaining doubts as to whether your plans are adequate and sound enough to guarantee success. You worry about the possibility of losing it all if your plans turn out not to be the most adequate or sound enough. And you entertain fears as to whether the plans will see you through any adversity. But this being America, you try to stay focused and not let such periods of doubt throw you offtrack, for this has the potential of creating a situation that could cause even a very sound plan to miscarry. Your resolve and determination in these moments will enable you to live through the doubts and transcend the mental difficulties and ultimately avoid the possibility of an overwhelming mental paralysis. In these moments, you often remind yourself that, in your newly adopted American culture, the line between the sound and the not-so-sound mind is so thin it could be nonexistent. You also remind yourself as often as you can that one of your primary responsibilities to yourself is to know when you are beginning to push too much too fast, particularly when the push is taking you way beyond your scope. And typical in American society, if you watch closely as it all plays around you, chances are a few rather unsavory incidents will serve as warnings, which may help you stay firmly grounded in your chosen course.

IKE C. UDEH

CHAPTER IV

What the System Has for You

ONE OF THE incidents that could remind you of the need to stay focused is tragedy. In your old culture, you witnessed tragedy. You witnessed death. You watched people in your community as they struggled in adversity, some pulling through and some not so lucky. You also watched marriages fail, though perhaps not nearly as frequently as in your newly adopted American culture. In your new culture, you witness death and the pain it brings to the bereaved. But you also notice that in your new culture, death seems to take on added significance and the societal approach to it appears to demonstrate a philosophical stance in conflict with itself. This stance plays out in various facets, which often mirror the inherent conflict within it.

First, you notice the concerted effort to banish death. You realize it is a subject not readily discussed, but you are aware of the understated attempt to entertain it as an inevitable occurrence which awaits everyone. And something tells you this is a forced acceptance, impossible to discountenance because of its unavoidable inevitability. This attempt to banish death is underscored by the intense medical undertakings aimed at conquering death and the instance of dying. The attempt at banishment, you are made aware of, centers on another societal approach to death, which is denial. You witness some of the goings-on around you, and you get the impression that there is an undercurrent of a wish that betrays the American tendency to view death as an incident that can be effectively kept at bay and, thus, create the possibility of lessening the impact of its finality. Of course, this instance of amelioration is only too transparently illusory, though the illusion therein is comfortably accommodated. And, no, you do not condemn this practice. You do not, for it serves the useful purpose of sustaining your efforts in whatever be your occupation and the hustle for toys. The practice, therefore, seems to guarantee an uninterrupted hustle, which increases your chances of success. And besides, since death is a sure thing, why let its certainty consume your life if in the end it's going to end your life anyway?

Then there is the societal drive to overcome death. This aspect of the culture becomes one of those you notice everyone around you loves to practice. First, the folks start by working as hard as they can on their bodies to counteract the process of dying, which is typified by aging. And you notice the generous supply of tools designed to aid you in this exercise, most of these made available on the shelves of various stores. And thanks to the mind-numbing competition among the various manufacturers, the sight and variety of these products almost guarantee their absolute effectiveness. And if in the end these products do not work for you or you simply do not feel like bothering with them, you are assured of the availability of other tools, albeit more drastic, which for your money will remove any marks carved on your person by time and the impact of its passage. So you find that the folks can go through a process of carving parts of the body, which reverses the damage done on them by nature. There is perhaps nothing really wrong with this practice, for in the end, you realize that it satisfies a societal need for youthful appearance. Let's face it, one sure way to postpone death and the process of dying is to stay permanently young. You can hardly lose sight of this very American cultural propensity, for while some are getting carved, some are adding a tool or two, often neatly placed in strategic positions to augment some delicate personal items. This way, these personal items are guaranteed to announce your presence.

You can hardly find fault with these practices, particularly in a culture that sets the human pace and determines the standard for overcoming everything that appears to diminish humanity's belief in its superiority to other animals. It is not that easy to lose sight of your new culture's approach to the various ways humankind can overcome mortality, which, with certainty, remains, just as it has always remained, beyond its control. You witness another aspect of the culture, which appears to invite death by courting it. You may even find yourself admiring this practice, so much so that you very willingly begin to participate in it. You take what in your previous culture could be considered unnecessary risk.

After all, there is no unexpected risk in that which is consciously and calculatedly undertaken, though it is a risk nonetheless; but the appearance of inherent/mystifying danger is mitigated by a refrain that often underlies the traveler's mental inclinations:

> There is nothing mysterious about everything;
> But everything mysterious about *nothing*!

And just in case it slips through his mind, the traveler cuddles the thought that

> There is a being in every traveler;
> And a traveler in every being.

So he quietly guides his mind as he considers the variety of persons who constitute this group, this distinct group, often referred to as humans, collectively called humanity. The traveler considers the nature of this group and weighs the significance of its existence. It is one that is

> Admired for its apparent uniqueness,
> And extolled for its alarming mentality;
> It is dignified for its dynamic existence,
> And glorified for its unique essence;
> It is glamorized for its wondrous skills,
> But betrayed by its monstrous deeds.

As he further deliberates, the traveler tries to look beyond the immediate shortcomings of this group but couldn't help the instances that mark the diminishment that goes with the nature of this group: humanity.

> Its place is exulted by its position,
> But damned by its disposition;
> And, yes, humanity,
> Blessed with longevity,
> But imbued with temporality.

Death in your new culture can also be an ugly final judgment rendered on the folks by murder. And this remains a supremely American cultural phenomenon that is difficult to explain. Not only were you surprised, just as most of the resident folks are, at the frequency of this incident, but you were also at a loss when you heard the term serial killer. Besides its ugliness and the degradation suggested by its occurrence, its very presence in a supposedly very highly civilized community makes you wonder at the prospects of humankind. At times, you may even find yourself wondering if civilization at its height, of necessity, begins to fold inward in a process of self-destruction. You become somewhat dismayed. But you cannot honestly blame it all on the resident folks because they are just as recent here as you are, except you are more recent. Also, you are a member of the community; hence, you are a part of the culture. If there is going to be a solution to this, then you'd better start thinking fast because everyone is expected to wear their thinking hat when it comes to social issues, and that includes you.

And now the traveler, not exactly thinking but perhaps only appreciating moments of thoughts as they drift, play, and fade just at the outskirts of his mind. They seem to resurface again and, rather, fading again. Then, they drift; and as if toying with his mind as they trace themselves just beyond the grasp of his mind, they fade. But it seems the traveler's got a slight hang of it; it is responsibility, both personal and social, including the capacity and willingness to realize the critical importance of it in any human society.

In the American society, it is almost as if death due to natural causes is an aberration, something that shouldn't happen to anyone in your new culture. Perhaps in your previous culture death was seen as an inevitable instance within the scope of human existence. It was embraced and accepted not necessarily as an end but an instance in a continuum. You may reflect on a common thought that obtains in both cultures with regard to death. In either case, death is accepted as an occurrence beyond human control. In your previous culture, just like this one, there are various ways the folks try to deal with death. The difference here becomes one of degree and intensity. Each culture utilizes the tools available to it. Invariably, the more advanced the culture, the more concentrated and intense its efforts. The difference in approach and mind-set between both cultures becomes a significant philosophical approach that defines the way the folks deal with death.

In this your new culture, the perceived capabilities of humankind, including the eminence attributed to it, creates a tantalizing factor that suggests an entitlement to immortality. There is the added element of abundance with regard to resources, which in turn renders human life so attractive it seems necessary to remove death and the instance of dying from the community. This aspect of the culture, including the process of its practical application, may seem futile and pretentious. But in the ultimate, it becomes a system of coping that helps the folks deal with an occurrence that remains absolute and unavoidable.

As your assimilation progresses, you gradually begin to focus more on the daily activities you have to do and less on the various aspects of the culture, particularly those that seem at odds with your perspectives. You begin to define what works for you as an individual. You proceed to learn how to find those things and how to apply them to the course of your daily life. But the American system nearly always has a way of either aiding you in your endeavors or effectively deflating your spirits and, thereby, undermining your aspirations. In such instances, your resolve and mental strength may help you to sustain your efforts and stay on track. But even then, there is no guarantee that you will successfully overcome what the system throws at you. And this is an aspect of your new culture that creates a doubt that often sits somewhere in your mind irrespective of how much you've achieved or at what point you are in your assimilation.

According to its detractors, this is another aspect of the American culture that renders it sterile and plastic and ultimately exposes its perceived attraction as deceitful seduction.

But the traveler wonders, is this really true?

You find that everyone is concerned about this aspect of the culture that has the ability to always leave a feeling of insecurity in your consciousness. You are nearly always being cognizant of the fact that whatever your place in the society and however much you have acquired, you stand just as good a chance of losing it all at any moment. You get the worrisome feeling that you are never really safe, at least not safe enough to effectively assuage your fears. You also notice there is an abundance of things around you, any one of which could do you in at any moment. And just about when you are doing all you can to transcend those fears, you realize it is a social phenomenon and you are not alone in your fears. Now you sense the very present factor of paranoia—so present in some instances it feels palpable.

Perhaps the fact that this social phenomenon is experienced by practically everyone has the tendency to lessen its impact on the individual, but you still have to deal with it and find your own ways of coping with it. As the folks will often tell you, as realistic as these fears may be, you don't let them overwhelm you. Some would even go so far as to tell you that you have only fear itself to fear, but none of these encouraging words has the ability to really remove these fears and doubts from the culture. Paranoia, it seems, is a very human attribute and, by logical extension, American.

Some of its detractors claim that your newly adopted American culture has a built-in mechanism that either strips you of what you've acquired or negates its beauty and diminishes its worth. Some of the proponents of the culture, however, will contend that it is this very aspect of the culture that affirms their unwavering belief in the system because it speaks to the brevity of life and crystallizes the inherent transiency of human existence. And ultimately, they claim, it encourages the individual to make the most of it while he can.

Now you begin to wonder exactly where you stand and precisely how to proceed.

It's not impossible anyway to fish yourself out of your fix. You take what you know and couple it with that which appeals to you and form your own opinion. You let the pundits do their stuff; after all, they too are all fated to go through the same ordeal. Their debate about what's right and what's wrong, in the end, becomes another way for them to preoccupy themselves with what they know is human dilemma.

As you ponder over the issue of aging and dying in the American culture, you also find that another issue of great interest is romance. This topic is of great interest here, not only because it plays out differently in every culture you visit but also because it takes on some very interesting formats in your new culture. Romance in the American culture becomes something of an enigma, particularly for those folks like you who were raised in some of those systems in which romance is defined by the family for the individual. In those systems, the family finds your mate and the two families huddle together to plan the union. According to folks in your new culture, this approach creates a system in which the union is not based on love but on familial necessities. They contend that without having love as the primary reason for the union, the couple only become tools whose sole importance in the community is centered on procreation. They become functional elements designed to guarantee the continuation of the family and the community at large. These detractors also claim that this system often leaves the individuals in the union essentially silent with regard to the formulation of an enterprise that demands their lives, their emotions, their energy, and the totality of their being.

You suspect that there could be some merit to these claims, especially since this system of forming a union of two different individuals essentially sees the romantic choices of the individual not as the primary determining factor but only secondary to family and communal needs. This factor, when coupled with the difficulties and issues that are inherent in these unions, makes this system rather difficult to embrace. But the proponents of the system point to its endurance and, consequently, its ability to better sustain the couple in times of adversity. They cite the frequency of divorce in your newly adopted American culture as another reason for which their system is better.

But as the traveler wrestles with this apparent dichotomy, he seems to appreciate the fact that in all cultures, a union between two humans always has its difficult angles. This appears to be an inherent factor just as romantic moments of wholesome togetherness seem to be a critical fabric of its success.

But you wonder, is it really better? In substance, what's so admirable about a marital union, glued together by familial demands, sustained by communal expectations, but lacking the preeminence of individual mental and sentimental gratifications?

Do those cultures that practice marital unions not primarily based on love and romance see love in this practice? You wonder! If so, how true and significant is such love since its basic structure arises from and is couched on a preplanned and predetermined course decided by others and anointed by the community at large?

The traveler weighs this point and wades through the intricate web of its implications. There seems to be no perfect answers but not exactly devoid of some answer/s, sufficiently adequate to offer a plausible statement that begins to address an answer.

And that brings you to the way romance plays out in your new culture. The first thing you might notice is that it appears romance is totally the individual's choice and how it is carried out is up to the individual. You find this to be another aspect of the culture that emphasizes the individual rather than the community. As seen by its proponents, this guarantees true emotional attachment and, consequently, the willingness to make a commitment that is based on the choice of the individual. But you are somewhat hesitant to buy into this, though it sounds logical and romantically appealing. Seen from the theoretical standpoint, this system appears to be reasonable, ideal, and romantically attractive. It seems to suggest a system capable of creating an atmosphere perfect for forming a union. The overriding factor here is love—romantic love as it proponents claim. You also notice the abundance of messages within the community that utilize romantic love as the catch for whatever is being offered or promoted. You hear the folks talk about it so often that you begin to realize that wallowing in the topic itself, not necessarily the practice, appears to satisfy the romantic needs of some of the folks. Perhaps they would rather live with the safety and satisfaction guaranteed in the abstractions of romance than deal with the difficulties involved in actual romantic relationships. Such preferences could be an inclination for emotional safety as a consequence of experiential necessity.

At this point of your assimilation, it is likely that your comparison of the two cultures, the American and your previous culture, with regard to romance is not only helping you to determine your own approach to this aspect of the culture but also aiding you in the process of finding the most satisfying grounds on which to anchor your feelings and emotions, if or when you find yourself on the threshold of a romantic activity. On the other hand, you may already be in a romance and only trying to sort out all the intricacies. As it so often happens, romance in your new culture can come your way shortly after your arrival and, for some, the opportunities of a romance find them quicker than they are prepared for. Unfortunately, a good number of these folks become victims of a system of romance that lies outside the scope of their definition of a romance. They've learned upon arrival, or even before, that the American culture, in all its practical forms, encourages romance or a semblance of it. The culture creates an atmosphere that makes romance, particularly between two individuals, a necessity. This aspect of the culture, through the implications of its drive for individuality, necessitates romance. It glorifies it. It promotes it. The culture makes romance so desirable that you may begin to get the message that your life would be damned and so miserable as to totally lack any bright points, if you don't have romance in your life.

It is often only a matter of time, a brief time mostly, for you to notice that it is very beneficial for you to find a partner. You soon learn that there are various consequences of being a loner, and these can affect the individual in various ways with various impacts. And some of these consequences can be such that you get the feeling it is the society passing judgment on you for being a loner. As a loner, you are seen as an oddball. You could be defined as somewhat weird and sometimes as a different person. It is as if your neighbors regard you as a social misfit who either doesn't have the romantic inklings or simply doesn't have the guts to muster the courage for a romantic enterprise. You could even be seen, depending on how extreme your aloneness is, as the unfriendly loser to be avoided definitely by the local kids if not by all. Yours becomes such that it appears there is something about your person that plays against the social norm.

So you feel that it not only behooves you to find romance as a resident in America, but it also becomes necessary, at least for your own emotional survival. As you consider romance, you also wonder what it could hold in store for you. You've seen and heard so much of the horror stories arising from various romances—both the good and the bad ones. You witness some of the games played in the supposedly good ones. You see how selfishness, self-centeredness, and meanness are redefined by the individuals who are romantically involved in order to accommodate what would otherwise be inexcusable behaviors from their partners; and often, you almost have pity on these folks as you watch them suffer as the romance ends at their own expense—both emotionally and financially. In such instances, it at times seems as if a greater majority of the victims are often male. Some of these folks are so badly broken that they literally drift through the day, their physical presence marked by a very obvious emotional absence. Unless you know the person, these folks often have difficulty interacting socially; and for some, it is as if they've unwittingly found themselves at the very limits of their sanity. You get the feeling it could only take the most trivial incident to nudge them over the edge. And incidentally, you don't fault these folks or pretend to revel in their discomfiture or entertain the thought that you are better at handling a romance than they did, for you know that you could be in their shoes at any moment.

Oh yes, the resident folks in America will always tell you that romance in your new culture is a game of conflicting experiences. It is an undertaking in which the very social factors that encourage it are the same ones that undermine it.

Individuality –
Be yourself and,
Define your needs;
Individuality –
Define your path and,
Find your road;
Individuality –
Find yourself and,
Fend for yourself
And
When the need arises,
Protect the self,
And
Damn the rest.

Now you wonder how easy it could possibly be to sustain a meaningful romantic relationship in such an atmosphere in which so many issues run into conflict with each other. Perhaps you proceed to try nonetheless. You try because it is a means for survival and you get involved because nature propels you toward a partnership with another human person.

Assuming you've had the opportunity of being in a romantic relationship in America, you may have the extra luck of feeling blessed by the success of your relationship or cursed as the recipient of a misfortune endowed upon your being and painfully manifested in the dislocation of your spirit. In the former case, you may find yourself measuring not exactly your luck but the lifespan of the romance, the incidence of luck notwithstanding. And this is just so because the measure of romantic success in your new culture is often determined by too many factors beyond the individual's control.

If you were among the unfortunate group, you find no comfort among others of the same fate. You may even be more inclined to seek to avoid them, for the mere association with them could appear to make your situation worse. It is as if you've found a miserable spot in the camp of romantic losers, which makes you a double loser. But if your case is somewhat extreme, you may find yourself among a company of losers whose approach to their plight is to wear it on their sleeves. These folks don't hesitate to tell you their stories when you encounter them, never mind they are unsolicited. It is as if they seek pity from any willing listener and distantly entertain the hope that you might point them toward a more successful romantic enterprise. And as the sun sets, these folks often gather at one of theirs to reminisce and ponder over what could or should have been. They sit in a circular formation, legs crossed and hunched over a little. Their arms cut through the air as they utilize personal gestures to emphasize their points. These gestures, it is said, often carry deeper meaning than the observer can see. It is believed that these gatherings often provide help, which apparently has been known to prevent some folks from going over the cliff.

To these persons, word has it that there is added relief from knowing that the facilitator, the one who usually runs the group, is an expert of sorts. To the uninitiated, this is the one whose experience was so severe you could almost feel it; and at times, this person has been through it more than once as to render him/her totally immune to the disastrous effects of a failed romance. So, being so seasoned, he finds himself a job preaching to a miserable group of romantic losers. Incidentally, this seasoned person is often one of those folks who will tell you that heaven helps those who help themselves. But you wonder exactly, how is heaven helping you when you are hanging out with a bunch of losers and listening to another? But this is America, and it's all okay!

As an individual in these matters of romance, you may want to sign up with those hardy souls in the outposts of rural America. For these folks, life is tough and nothing comes easy or taken for granted. You take what life throws at you, roll up your sleeves, and stride on. As far as they are concerned, life has no room for preaching and wallowing in the postmortem of a failed romance, especially not in America!

If you found romance with one of the resident folks, you not only have to worry about the problems, which are the natural by-products inherent in relationships, but you also have to worry about the culture clash, which becomes more pronounced in a romance. If yours is one with a person from your previous culture, your fate may depend mostly on luck and somewhat on the character of the individual with whom you are involved. In this case, there may be more instances to see eye to eye from the same cultural standpoint; and the possibility creates the opportunity for more meaningful communion since the nuances and implications of cultural perspectives could encourage a better understanding between the couple. In this instance, the commonality of cultural experiences becomes another bonding factor. But here, you are not exactly home free. You still have to deal with some natural problems. You have to deal with personal growth both social and mental, and this is precisely where more luck than character plays an important role.

The commonality of cultural experiences may be a strong and uniting element, and character may play an important role. But the American society has very strong forces that could play negatively on the prospects of your romance. There is also the factor of personal growth. As persons, you and your partner will grow individually, which often implies growing separately according to the person's manner of assimilation in the new culture. There is never a guarantee that you will both grow together along the same mental track and undergo identical changes. As such, you may now have the additional problem of finding yourself in a romantic partnership with one from a previous culture same as yours but with a rapidly changing perspective on both social and romantic issues. This may even prove to be a far more difficult ordeal to live with than the usual problems you'd otherwise encounter if you were romantically involved with one of the resident folks.

You may find that you and your partner are now beginning to define social and other cultural issues differently. What seemed very significant to both of you in a relationship may now seem less meaningful and, therefore, trivial to your partner. And as your partner finds available resources that could provide both economic and emotional support for him/her, you may find that as the "macho" male, you are no longer dictating the course of the relationship.

In such instance, as a male, your plight may be exacerbated if you are given to frequent bragging about your masterful control of your romantic relationship. This often applies to all the folks irrespective of their place of birth. These are often those among the folks who wallow in their perceived position as the one in control in a romantic relationship and their ability to direct it as they see fit. They are often impressed with themselves and often have no tolerance for anyone whom they consider incapable of carrying on a romance like they can. You will often be told, however, to disregard these folks and their bragging presence for, in most cases, theirs is only an instance of perceived control only deftly allowed to continue by the rather quiet partner who holds the leash. Some of these "macho" persons may experience an incident that might challenge their preferred beliefs and threaten their security but would dismiss it as only happening because they allowed it to—an example of their considered thoughtfulness in play. But by the time they realize the reality of their situation, theirs may be a story of a failed romance, and their agony is made more painful by the realization that they were not exactly in control all along. They were only wallowing in their illusions and essentially playing the second fiddle.

Some of these people would swear they had it right but only missed the goal by a step or two. But it is okay to let them maintain such thinking. After all, holding on to the residual tidings of a faded glory may be sufficient to sustain their spirits well beyond the glory. At this point theirs is a mental state in permanent transition.

Ultimately, your situation is your problem, and finding the solution to the problem is your responsibility. As you search for solutions to your problem, you find that blaming the American culture or whatever you feel is wrong with it can only be a distraction that could prevent you from focusing your energy as much as you should on solving your problem. In your efforts, some of the information you gathered before your arrival in America could be of use to you, and it may be vital to the successful resolution of the issues facing you. Some of these may be those aspects of your new culture that encourage transplanted people like you to fall back on systems from your previous culture that may be lacking in the new one. And since your problem centers on romance, you may do better relying on the support you can get from your own family, particularly if it is within reasonable distance for contact and immediate support. In this case, you are more inclined to rely more on your previous culture for rescue and mental support. Your previous culture becomes a wellspring that provides a much-needed ingredient to help you transcend your predicament. If you play it right, this could be a process you may have to utilize very often.

It may seem like straddling two cultures, but it is a process that comes into play when you need that extra resource that may be beyond your reach. If you were in a romance that has died, you'd be lucky if it simply faded out and your partner drifts off with a different concern, for in most cases, romances in America don't simply break up and ultimately die out. They enter a new phase in which you both face each other in a fight such that you've never experienced in the past and definitely never imagined you would find yourself in. It often does not matter if your partner was from the same culture as you or a person you met in your new culture. These fights can get downright nasty, and the more toys you'd acquired, the nastier it gets. If you are male, you'd better get down on your knees and say your prayers. It doesn't matter how saintly you had been. It doesn't matter how well you can show that your partner had been the aggressor and had an ulterior motive. All it takes is one wrong untrue story by your partner, and you are in for the fight of your life. Whether you approve of it or not, as a male, you are guilty at first sight; and if there is cause for giving the benefit of a doubt, you can bet it's not coming your way.

But you are happy with your newly adopted American culture and you are quite impressed by so much about the system that you become hesitant to believe some of the horror stories you've heard about these postromantic fights. And if it happens that you've been a victim in such ugly situations, you find yourself in a real quandary. Then you proceed to figure out why the culture in your new society is seemingly antimale. You do some research, and you ask questions, and that's when you get the all-too-generic answer: it's a male-bashing thing that started a while ago and this is the end product. Of course, you wonder, why is no one doing anything about it? And the folks tell you it's useless. The law is too heavily weighted against the men, and they are afraid of being labeled with the other really terrible word in the community—*sexist*—and one may ultimately be hopelessly written off as a chauvinist pig!

Perhaps you have been lucky not to have experienced any of these fights yourself, but you are familiar with some of those persons whose ill luck had brought such misfortune on their person. You may be inclined to feel empathy and sorry for them, particularly those whose experience played out in its nastiest form. You can't help but notice their pitiful look, often emphasized by an absent-minded mismatch of clothing. They interact socially all right but are quick to run for shelter at the mere salutation from a person from the opposite sex. They appear comfortable in an all-male setting but still wear a touch of fear that is no doubt generated by latent suspicion—a permanent scar from an ugly fight. Some of these folks will engage you in a conversation,

IKE C. UDEH

perhaps hoping to help another one of their kind stay clear of some of those dangerous curves. But some of them are often mostly silent and only saying very little, no doubt hoping that an obvious economy of words demonstrates the difficulty of communication in a romantic postmortem.

You may decide to go a little further with your research, which finds you at the doorstep of the local congressman. You've heard so much about this person, and you are aware of his latest promise how, in the name of fairness and decency, he would change things and push through a bipartisan something that would level the field. His actions would liberate the men, and true liberty and freedom would be theirs. But just before you take the next step, the neighbors may stop and remind you that it's a losing effort because your local politician will play only in accordance with political expediency. That's where you stop all actions because you know only too well that your stint with the politician was only an enlightening antecedence, which should remind you that the next figure you might wish to approach may have to weigh the exigency of the issue and your problems very likely may not meet the criteria for action. Perhaps you then become motivated to send a letter to some other political figure the folks say has been pretty loud lately. You are not exactly trying to put this person to the test of living up to his words; you only hope he could put the issue on the right track. You get a few words of advice from the neighbors, but you are cautious not to wrap your message up in excessive platitudes. Then you send your package, a nice little request designed to highlight the issue. You take care to make sure your message fits the moment. It is not too generously essayistic and, proper to the person and the nature of his utterances, the message is sufficiently cant and calculated to massage the ego and nourish a nascent dream for higher office. Then you sit back and wait for a response, during which time you might be better served if your hopes are less than optimistic, and your fingers are neatly crossed.

You'd be luckier if you got no response, for any answer you get is sure to leave you empty and baffled.

It may be within your luck to find a romance that holds true to what a healthy and nurturing relationship should be, and if this becomes the case for you, you hope and pray for its lasting endurance.

Despite the difficulties and issues that can plague your romance in America, it will be a disservice to focus on those aspects of your new culture that do not necessarily tell the whole story. There are other aspects of the culture, which make your newly adopted community worth the trip and a change of cultures. After all, you've just settled in a culture, which tells you that you are worth all the attributes blessed upon you by nature. It reminds you that you are a creation of whichever force, energy, or occasion that designed and brought the circumstance of your being into existence. The American culture states, rather unequivocally, that your person is an instance in the manifestation of humanity as an inviolate product of supreme excellence. You also note and appreciate the sustained preference for keeping it a truly classless society. After all, where else is it so possible to hail from the most humble background and live with the knowledge that any job, any position, is there for you to strive for, even running and directing the affairs of the entire country? And this is one aspect of your adopted American culture about which both its proponents and detractors find their thinking at a confluence.

There is also the ease with which you can assimilate, and this is so because the culture encourages you to do so; and there is an abundance of resources designed for you and others of your kind to make assimilation less demanding than it could otherwise be. As you begin to tap into the various opportunities available to you, you appreciate the accessibility and tools provided to aid you in your efforts. If your priorities are well defined, you find it much easier to work toward your objectives; and with an undercurrent of a strong sense of self, you feel comfortable with the thought that you are essentially the means and also the obstacle that could be in your own path. The focus of your efforts then becomes how far you wish to go in the pursuit of your dreams, and as long as the dreams are realistic, achieving them remains within the bounds of your capacities.

In the drive toward your goals, you may come across various issues, mostly social, that could stymie your plans. You will hear the residents talk about the various kinds of persons in your new community. You hear various words used in reference to each and every kind of person, some words employed to demean and ultimately discourage the individual from attempting to fully participate in the system. Depending on your background and ethnicity, some of these words can be offensively spat at you or surreptitiously placed in strategic positions as to get the most of your attention and do the most effective damage. Often the aim is toward the spirit because, if the motive is successful at this level, whatever is left of the individual is only a broken form, which becomes a personification of despair, despondence, and subservience. At times, some of these victims may top it all off with anger, which is always ready to explode and only being held together by a very thin thread of patience.

If your ethnicity falls within certain geographic areas, you are very likely to get some of these insulting languages coming your way. For those persons with these geographic backgrounds, experiencing these insults is practically inescapable. If there are other aspects of the American culture that are not the most desirable, the ethnic insults can be described as the most damnable aspect of the culture; and as you go about your business, you find that the intensity of its presence can vary from one place to the other. In your neighborhood and elsewhere, you hear the word *race* being used as a template on which the various persons in the society are categorized and placed in boxes designed to either enhance or diminish their persons.

Without being told, it soon becomes clear to you that these insulting words can be employed in such manner as to elicit various reactions from the victim. It could be used to elicit anger and, thus, move you to a fight. It could be employed to discourage your success by effectively breaking your spirits and thus paralyzing your efforts. And it could be employed in an attempt to diminish your worth by surreptitiously undermining your self-confidence. In all cases, however, the deed is destructive, the motive worthless, and the usage of such language degrades the quality of the culture and diminishes some of the more admirable qualities of the society as a whole.

As an individual in America, how you handle these instances of racial or ethnic insult becomes a key factor in treating it the way it should be treated. Yes, the law is there to help you deal with it when the insult or abuse is thrown at you; but besides that, your reactions to it can help you transcend its ugliness and rise above the perpetrator. To begin with, you know and the folks will tell you that it is a sure sign of an inferiority complex on the part of the abuser. It is also a telltale sign of insecurity and the unfortunate inability to maintain a decent social composure. And let's face it, every ethnic group has its beauties and also some less admirable qualities.

In your new culture, your primary role in this issue could be to join the forces of enlightenment and help to educate some of those persons who are often inclined to utilize insulting language on others. For these abusers, it might seem like a moment of triumph; but in actuality, it is a misguided attempt at addressing some of their own unresolved issues. In substance, you don't exactly turn the other cheek but you rise above the instance. You see it for what it's worth, and you calmly stay head and shoulders above the abuser. There is high esteem, there is class, and there is magnanimity about your presence when the other fellow is tactfully placed in his indecent place thereby letting his diminished person speak to his inadmirable presence.

Dealing with such rather difficult issues is an important part in the process of your assimilation in America. In the process of defining your goals and carving out your niche, you find various instances in which you have to negotiate in order to realize some of your goals. In this case, terms of negotiations become critically important. You may encounter situations in which you find some obstacles in your path, and after a thorough examination, you realize that these obstacles were thrown your way not by nature but by another person. This act could be out of envy or sheer malice. It could even be a calculated attempt to undermine your progress by throwing you off track. How you deal with such incidents will be determined by how prepared you are and how adept you are at sidestepping such obstacles and remaining focused on your plans. You'd also do better by reminding yourself that such human machinations are not unique to your new culture. You probably experienced worse situations in your previous culture. The difference here becomes one of intensity and the ultimate effect such activities have on you, and the impact of such activities in your new culture can be more devastating because the process of achieving your goals can be so expensive it's impossible to find your bearing after a derailment. And it is very likely that here in America, there are more toys at stake; and the more toys, the costlier the impact of any machinations planned against you.

There is, however, some recourse to you as a victim of such unfriendly acts. Again, this is another aspect of the American culture that sustains your drive and upholds your spirit. There is recourse for literally every victim and tools in the system that are often placed within reach to help the people address an unfair situation. There are also people within your community who would drop everything to help you deal with a difficult situation. In most cases, some of these willing helpers may not

IKE C. UDEH

even know you or care who the hell you are. The point is a person needs a helping hand, and they are very willing to jump in and help.

Without a doubt, this aspect of the culture that demonstrates some of the real nature of the American people is one of the most admirable qualities of the culture.

As a transplant, before your arrival in America, most of what you heard centered around money and the abundant possibilities you or anyone can tap into. Perhaps you heard a few things about the people and the way they interact with other people, and the tone of what you heard no doubt depended on the experiences of whoever made the information available to you. Chances are, you took the information with as much open-mindedness as everything else you heard; but as you experience the culture and its people, you begin to form your own opinion, which either corroborates what you heard or refutes it. Now, as you form your own opinion, you have firsthand experience to aid you, and what you ultimately end up with depends on the nature of your experiences and how the culture impacts you.

No doubt, one of the factors that may impact you the most could be what you experience as you interact with the people in your new culture. The interpersonal interactions that happen as you go about your daily activities will begin to create a new perspective that begins to define how you choose to relate to others. It will underlie both the social and personal relationships and even shape some of the terms in any romantic relationship. You will encounter some of the most considerate persons you can possibly meet, and you will meet some folks who will make you wonder how it could be possible for nature to bring about such individuals. The activities of some of these persons will make you question the propriety of courteous and respectful interactions with others, and some could even make you wonder how much hope there is for humanity. One of the dangers here is to use such persons as a yardstick for judging the community as a whole; and because in some areas of the society there seems to be a predominance of these, the temptation to make such judgment is pretty strong. However, even in these areas, you will still come across some of the nicer people who will no doubt make you feel there is a redemptive chance for humanity.

You may be lucky to find yourself among the more enlightened people about whom you get the feeling they have more important things to worry about instead of trying to define their lives according to how much nastiness and impoliteness they can muster as they interact with others.

But as in every society, you find a common thread that tends to give you a fairly good picture of the people within it. In your new society, there is an overriding inclination to help one's neighbor, particularly in times of real adversity or overwhelming disaster. This measure of kindness is often more evident when the help is intended to benefit strangers at a distance. In such cases, you feel there is greater satisfaction derived from anonymity when the recipient does not know the donor. In times of disaster, the great outpouring of both emotional and material support becomes another facet of the American culture that demonstrates that even in the face of individualism, people can still find the ability to reach out in support of others. And this is where you wonder, does the individual donor feel some relief from a sense of guilt perhaps associated with having too many toys? Or does the donor feel duty bound as a result of a latent sense of social responsibility to help a neighbor in times of hardship? You can't help but consider the case when the help, as a collective national deed, is designed to bring relief to folks miles away in other parts of the world. In such cases, particularly when the deed is untainted by political expediency, you certainly admire what in the American culture stands as a moment of triumph for humanity.

As you admire such deeds of kindness, you still may encounter some people who are adamantly opposed to such deeds, especially when they are destined for people outside the country. These people who oppose such deeds often won't hesitate to share their views, even though they run counter to the more widespread opinions shared by the greater generality of the American people. And this is quite OK too, for it satisfies that aspect of the culture, which welcomes and accommodates dissent. And because nothing in the culture forces you to share any one particular view on any issue, you appreciate the privilege of being a part of a system of debate, dissent, and consent. You appreciate this facet of American culture also because you witness how much enlightenment such privileges provide in the society and you are aware of how such instances of enlightenment encourage free thinking and, consequently, advancement.

Your admiration for the kindness shown by some of the people in your new society may not necessarily be complete without some drawback. You often find that in some instances, depending on your background particularly with regard to ethnicity and the area in which you happen to be located, you may end up getting persecution instead of help in times of difficulty. In such cases, the persecution may come as a faceless enemy, in which case you wonder if such incidents could be systemic. As you consider the nature of such practices and why it may at times seem systemic, you suspect that this may not exactly be the more common practice.

That's when you proceed to isolate one cultural example of kindness from one of indecent human behavior, and you are somewhat inclined to suspect there is something that is not totally American about that which is definitely abhorrent; and this momentary mental exercise provides the opportunity for you to consider all the variables.

And ultimately, you are able to place that which is not the most admirable in the isolated narrowness of its obvious inelegance.

PART TWO

CHAPTER V

A World View

THERE IS A perception about your newly adopted American society, which is not exactly shared by the world at large, which is that it is a society of affluence, waste, and excess. This perception may not be entirely correct, but viewed from other parts of the world, your new society appears to have so much at its disposal that the folks don't have a good understanding of what it means to be poor or live in destitution. And as the outsiders see it, without a real sense of hardship, it is impossible to truly appreciate life with its limitations. With such a view, it becomes rather easy to dismiss your new society's philosophy of life as inadequate and lacking the experiential factors necessary for a complete approach to human existence in all its various facets. As the Americans will tell you, this is an incorrect perception, which in some cases is generated by envy and the lack of firsthand experience of this society. Some of the people may point to those other societies in which the enormity of natural resources provides so much wealth for every individual in the community that it is literally impossible to imagine poverty let alone grasp its implications. These are some of those communities in which you could rightly say all that glitters is truly gold. In these communities, life is defined in accordance with what is available to the inhabitants and that includes wealth, pain, and losses of every kind. Ultimately, people say, in every human community, life is defined according to the way it impacts the people.

Besides the availability of resources, which is more widespread in your new community than other places, there is also the politics, which has a way of affecting literally every community in the world. And as you go from one place to the other, the politics of your new society may play differently in one place than in another. In some places, the politics, to the individual, may seem hostile and unfriendly while in others it may seem cordial and accommodating, even tolerant. Here again, you find that the determining factor is expediency, and the conflict arises from the fact that what may seem expedient to one society may be hostile to the other.

Invariably, you are bound to form your own opinion, especially since you are now resident in this society and are a member of your community; and as you assimilate, the view from the outside world becomes less a determining factor. Now you are faced with responsibilities, both personal and social. You have priorities that are no longer defined by your old culture but determined by circumstances that have become intrinsic parts of your daily activities in America. And because these circumstances help to determine your priorities, they tend to lend credence to your perceptions, your choices, your decisions, and the utility of your actions. And since your thinking is now grounded on the principles of the freedom of thought and expression, you are now more likely to engage in a personal debate regarding your own view of your new society. Whatever views you held before you arrived in America become subject to reassessment. You are now thinking within the parameters of concrete experiences and beginning to reason yourself into systems of belief that are based on practical experiences.

Essentially, you are searching for answers within various sets of applicable paradigms.

In the end, as a transplanted individual, you may be less inclined to be overly critical of some of the aspects of the American culture. Of course, you may not approve of everything that impacts you. You may even dislike some of the things that either by design or default fall along your path and have the potential of impeding your progress. And you may still find occasion to entertain some negative views about some things in your new culture because, as you go about your daily business, you will encounter unpleasant situations. How some of such situations affect you will definitely depend on their nature and intensity.

In this society, opinions about life, people, nature, and everything that dwells within it vary as you go from one geographic area to another. These opinions are often colored by the political leanings and, at times, the religious beliefs of the individual. Depending on the individual, people's opinions could sometimes be rather dogmatic. They can be very passionate and so strongly held that they allow no room for debate. When you encounter people with such strong opinions, often on social issues, you can't fail but notice their unfriendly nature and propensity for rather distasteful social interactions. With such persons, you often wonder where the pain lies. And as you witness their indecorous attitude, you suspect that there is a rather serious personal deficit at play. Such people are not only seeking to compensate by vehemence the lack of reasoned conviction but apparently feel the need to impose their opinion on you. Your encounter with such very opinionated people often leaves you feeling appreciative of any opportunity for dialogue. The experience also crystallizes the importance of social decorum and underscores the criticality of collogue as a function of social interactions. This holds true, particularly in interactions based on reason and buoyed by the sheer decency of mutual respect. In these interactions, there is a quiet communion of intellect that negates the difficulties at points of conflict.

At times, you'd do much better by avoiding situations that may create an encounter with such people. You may run into people like these often, but it becomes more unfortunate when you encounter them in places you'd least expect to find them, such as among those folks you might consider enlightened. In such situations, the manners of these rather inconsiderate people seem more disgusting as they are made more apparent against the backdrop of the enlightened presence of others. It is often at such moments that you wonder if such uncouth people are everywhere. And if you've been unfortunate enough to have encountered them rather too often, you might be inclined to think theirs is not simply an aberration but the norm, particularly since your perceptions are beginning to lend a quotidian element to their behavior. But as in all situations, you take what is being thrown at you, place it in its proper context, and dispose of it appropriately. In this case, you let it ride and, ultimately, drift into the inconsequentiality of its uselessness. And, yes, it's quite OK to let these types of persons drift along with their unpleasant attitude. After all, the nastiness of their manners is just as disgusting as their sickening presence.

Just as you may encounter the unfriendly people, you are equally likely to encounter the supposedly pious, whose persons appear to thrive on the personal belief that they have been chosen by goodness knows who to preach and pray for the conversion of your being. Most of these folks will tell you about the unworthiness of your person and the danger faced by your being of eternal damnation. In most cases, you do not argue with them, for there is always something dogmatic about their presence, including an air of ordained piousness about their person. It is as if their very presence has been anointed with transcendent powers as to guarantee immediate redemption to those who'd be patient and willing enough to listen to their preaching. Of course, you have to exude a particular attribute of instant credulity and your mind, demonstrably malleable, your presence very accommodating and adorned with the graciousness of very obvious humility. With such presence, you are no threat and you are not immediately perceived as the difficult type who might prove less welcoming and thus beyond redemption. You are seen by these preachers as the willing type whose being is ready to take in the word and see the light toward salvation.

With these chosen people, your religious inclinations are immaterial and your beliefs as an individual are not important. They possess an all-encompassing right that supersedes whatever beliefs you might hold, and this qualifies them not simply as the chosen few but also the blessed, whose earthly mission is to rid the world of undesirables and cleanse the meek in preparation for eternal life.

After an encounter with these preachers, you are often left wondering just why all these days you haven't been able to define human existence in accordance with their mission. And at times, if you nurture strong religious inclinations that are in opposition to theirs, you are left feeling insulted and a tad angry at them or upset at yourself for not vehemently standing up for your beliefs. Or you might just be the nonbeliever, the staunch atheist whose mental preoccupation is the very ardent wish to unravel the intricacies of human existence. In this case, you are, like the preachers, on a mission, which is equally aimed at the redemption of humanity. Your mission might seem different from that of the preachers, but it is a mission nonetheless. And from the perspective of those who might share your views, your mission might hold more benefit for humankind, particularly since it is designed to unravel the mysteries and complications surrounding human existence. And ultimately, the success of your mission may not only be redeeming from mental bondage for humanity but also providing explanations capable of removing the specter of nothingness and enabling humanity to come to terms with its own existence.

In any case, you still appreciate a culture that not only accommodates varying points of view but also encourages and welcomes debate in practically all areas of human interaction.

But as you wallow in your moment of appreciation of some aspects of the American system, you also consider the politics of the people. You witness the different views from the varying political camps and watch the gamesmanship, the machinations, the studied unctuous presence, and the borrowed persona garbed in pretentious humility. Then you listen to the rhetoric, steeped in insincere platitudes and delivered through the parted lips of practiced smiles. But you may not be sickened by all that you hear or see because among these champions of political gamesmanship are the fairly sincere ones who feel a special calling not just to run for an office but also expose what they see as the falsity and deception characterizing the general politics. These opponents of the apparent status quo, however, remain on the periphery of the main political arena; and their voices are often given minimal exposure, which limits their reach.

But you will be sickened by some rhetoric that spills with venom and aims to destroy and damage. These are some of the worst statements often made by some politicians, and these statements come with slash and burn as their trademark. And as you watch the practitioners of such politics, you begin to wonder just where politics end and hate begins. In some of these speeches, you feel the palpable presence of hate and intolerance. You find yourself at a loss to define the practitioners as honest politicians and you suspect that some of them are natural haters for whom politics provide a safe arena for them to display their unfortunate attributes. You feel truly sickened by these types of politicians; and the more you watch and listen to them, the more you wonder precisely how such minds work. At this point, you are no longer watching politics but watching hate spilling all around; and as you feel the hate, you wonder at what point did the individual pick up the distasteful habit of speaking with such venom. But something tells you humans do not really come with so much venom, which makes you wonder at what point did the envenomation of this individual occur. Was it through an exogenous process of an unfortunate environmental misfortune or a regrettable instance of an accident at birth?

Whatever your findings, it is difficult for any truly concerned individual to be at peace with this process because he is now left with a latent sense of discomfort knowing that such a hateful person could and has been known to win an important political office.

Perhaps your only recourse here is the knowledge that the ultimate power still lies with the people who can choose to vote him out of office. And that's another instance of enlightenment that lends beauty to the culture.

As in most other parts of the world, politics in the American society plays in accordance with the prevailing culture, and as you go from one place to another, you find that the politics tend to reflect local sentiments. But there is a general trend that runs through politics on a national level, and this is the one person one vote process in a representative system. This system is by no means perfect, but its very idea and practice lend hope to a process of human social intercourse. But unfortunately, this otherwise brilliant and creative approach to government is often debased by the politicians themselves. Viewed in comparison with that of some other places in the world, the system of governing in the American society remains exceedingly attractive and worthy of emulation. It's not simply the appeal of its democratic process but essentially the consistency and fairness legislated into the process that makes the system exemplary.

As you dig deeper into the politics and governing process, however, you find traces of inbuilt factors that allow room for manipulation according to the whims of the individual politician or a section of the community in its attempt to either exclude or disfranchise another segment of the community. At times, in some locales, such practices appear to be commonplace and rather openly done. In such cases, a sense of fairness may move you to sympathize with the disfranchised. But that may depend on your ethnic or geographic background, which may not only make you a sympathizer but also a potential victim. In most instances, you find systems designed to prevent these practices. You may also find a communal effort aimed at providing relief to the disfranchised, a sort of disencumberment that ameliorates their discomfort. But as with most handouts in this society, this otherwise noble deed of providing help to those who need it has a social stigma that does not necessarily diminish its worth but makes the recipient look more like a failure than a victim of disfranchisement. After all, you are expected to fend for yourself. You are expected not to depend on others or on the society. You are expected to succeed, your misfortunes notwithstanding. And there is little room for tolerance for those who are perceived as playing the victim role in a dog-eat-dog society where everyone is seen as the architect of his own fortune. The disconcerting implication here is that, conversely, everyone invariably becomes the architect of his own misfortunes, the nature of those misfortunes notwithstanding.

But beyond the social perceptions, there are those in the American society who are true victims through a misguided social program, an unfortunate ethnic/racial disfranchisement, or a deliberate relocation that ultimately proves to be a dislocation of a segment of the society through a regrettable process of ethnic deracination.

Such unfortunate treatment of some segments of the population by some politicians could still be noticed though with the silent blessing of the voters. Despite such practices, however, it is often gratifying to note that a greater generality of those who relocate to your newly adopted society like you did do so not simply for the opportunities but also for a system of governance that offers hope to every individual. And such gratifications become an affirmation of your own decision to relocate.

Did you lose sight of your primary reasons for relocating? Or are you now caught up in the daily grind, the daily hustle, and the relentless drive for the acquisition of toys? Perhaps you are still appropriately focused on your priorities and calculatedly unencumbered with the seductive gratifications of plastics, in which case you are almost a social phenomenon. If, per chance, you've been able to sidestep the lore of plastics, those things coveted as credit cards, and keep your financial activities within the limits of your pocket, then you have truly achieved a remarkable feat. You have resisted one of the most seductive social temptations that is so perfectly packaged with an aura of existential necessity that you are inclined to view your life as worthless without them.

The purveyors of these items would swear they serve useful needs in the society; they'd insist that they are a necessary part of your financial and economic success. But in actuality, are credit cards a critically important factor in your financial and economic well-being? You may not want to take this question to a lender in your local bank!

Your adopted American society offers a lot and has the potential of taking a lot from you. Often, it is not only that which you consciously aim to contribute as a measure of social responsibility that is taken from you but also some of those things you would rather not part with. An example of this is in times of economic downturn when you are compelled to give up your time for yourself and your sense of worth, including some of your hard-earned money, such as when you are forced to work for much lower wages than were originally promised you. Or when you have to give up a couple or more paychecks in order to retain your job. In these instances, you are forced by circumstances of survival to contribute not only to the survival of your employer but also to the improvement of the economy in general. As you make such sacrifices, you may be dismayed to find that those at the top in your company are being given so many raises and benefits that you find it difficult to comprehend. But your dilemma doesn't end there. You now find yourself frustrated at what you see as economic unfairness. For some folks, the frustration increases for every minute they have to spend at work, and it eventually becomes directed inward. The personal and social implications of this problem are not very difficult to see. As an individual, you may choose to raise your voice against such injustice. But you soon realize how extremely powerless you are in the scheme of things, and this brings the message home to your sense of survival: you take what you get and try to ruffle no feathers in order to guarantee some measure of economic survival.

As an individual, you may agree that it is fair to say that there are some employers who would strive to treat you better even when times are hard for the employer. There are not too many of these employers, and you can count yourself lucky if you find yourself working for one.

As in most things in American society, you may find that you can be given the opportunity to renegotiate the terms of a contract to which you are signatory. And this could be anything from an employment contract to one that is between you and another individual or other persons. With such opportunities for renegotiation, you find it possible to do business with others on various levels of social and economic standing. This further adds to the possibility already in place for you or anyone else to create and start his own business. And if you so decide, you'll find resources that are put in place to enable you to grow your business. Such opportunity makes it possible for the individual to create a life for himself that is not economically dependent on others, and as long as he plays according to the ground rules, he can work himself to any economic success level he has set up as a goal.

As a transplant, whatever be your occupation in America, the goal remains the same: you strive to fend for yourself with the implicit belief that the only sure entity you can absolutely depend on is yourself. And this means you have to believe in yourself and trust that your capabilities are not just simply adequate but sufficiently adequate for the task at hand with some extra to tide you over those difficult moments when you need something beyond the merely adequate to survive. In deciding to be your own employer, by choice, you also decide to shoulder all the responsibilities that come with owning your own business; and these include the legal, financial, personnel, social, etc.

So along with the freedom of being your own boss, there is also the enormous responsibility of knowing that everything lies on your shoulders; and this ultimately means both the success and failure of your business. Also, like everything else in America, as you celebrate the arrival of a new patron or customer for your enterprise, you also anticipate the coming of a troublemaker with a summons in his pocket or something rather nefarious in his mind. And you guessed it, without this cultural phenomenon the term *dog eat dog* wouldn't be entirely very fitting. Could this be another facet of the American culture that diminishes any semblance of humanity in the social consciousness? The detractors of this society and its culture would say it not only negates humanity but also precludes any honest attempt at it.

By the time you are setting up a business, your assimilation must have reached an appreciable level of comfort, which includes a good knowledge of the culture, the people and the system, and how it works. Chances are you've also learned a few social skills that help you to deal with a few rather unpleasant social situations.

Ultimately, as a transplant, as you set up your own business, you find a way to manage and run it; and the results you get would depend on how much effort you put into it, including a measure of luck. This brings you back to the point about your background as an individual. In some cases, you may find it much easier to run your business with success if your ethnic background meets the environing social sentiments. And this is where a little luck goes a long way toward your success. But even when social conditions do not appear to be in your favor because of your ethnicity, you could still find ways to do business successfully. A lot of that would depend on how adept and diplomatic you are in managing both your personal and business affairs. It also helps to know that even in a not-so-friendly environment, you could still find some people who simply do not care who you are or bother themselves about your ethnicity. Such folks would work with you and would often stand with you in times when you face discrimination.

Dealing with difficult social situations, particularly those that involve interactions with others, is something you may have to do quite often. But as you learn the skills, you find it easier to handle such situations. And that may help to counter some of the racial/ethnic prejudices you may experience in the process of running your own business.

Your situation may be such that your occupation revolves around academics, in which case your focus will be centered on activities that are fairly removed from the immediate impact of discrimination, particularly in terms of ethnicity. But like most things in accord with the American system, you may still experience unpleasant social/racial situations that you'd least expect to find in this area of occupation.

At this point, you are beginning to find that this is an advanced society with equal measure of unpleasant social occurrences, which you may find impossible to explain. This dilemma becomes more disconcerting as you realize that unpleasant social incidents are inherent fabrics of the culture. But you spend little time in trying to resolve the issue for yourself because, by now, you've probably experienced various unpleasant social incidents such that you've come to expect it one way or another in varying degrees. Despite your familiarity with these social situations, however, you may still feel hurt and definitely unhappy when you encounter an unpleasant social incident, particularly when it is directed at you. Your familiarity with these incidents, in the end, may not necessarily immunize you against the discomfort of their impact. And in this case, it is not exactly your responses that dictate your feelings but the knowledge that, in spite of its advancement, the American culture, either by design or default, appears to cultivate instances of inter-ethnic discord.

You may try to discountenance the incidence of discrimination in the society and focus on the more positive aspects of the culture, but this may prove to be very difficult to do since both the good and the not-so-pleasant aspects of the culture are often interwoven. This makes it rather difficult not to notice those social incidents that you'd prefer to avoid. You'll often find that practically every aspect of your daily life

IKE C. UDEH

is affected one way or another by social occurrences that might seem removed from you. This holds true, especially since your activities, both private and social, are predicated on the fact that you cannot function totally independently from others in the community. Even if you are inclined to be a social isolate, the daily activities of your life as an individual are expressly connected to the activities of others. It is a critical interdependence that sustains the individual's subsistence.

But as you wonder about the not-so-pleasant aspects of the American culture and wade through the intricate fabrics of its fundamental basis, you find yourself in search of words sufficiently adequate to lend reason to your experience; and the more you search, the deeper your dilemma. But you are a member of the society and a part of the culture. So you are not exactly looking in from the outside and trying to solve a riddle from which you are removed but trying to find explanations for incidents that can only be brought into reality through the individual person.

So the problem you are trying to solve becomes an unpleasant incident that can only be brought to its practical manifestation through your person as an individual.

And as you delve further into your search, you begin to create comfortable mental situations that may enable you to find answers. You find yourself trying to escape from the total picture. You create a mental disposition that places you not within the confines of the culture but on the threshold of a neutral standpoint. But still you are no closer to any answers because what you are dealing with is a societal behavior as a function of an inherent cultural phenomenon. Now you suspect it is a social destiny with its critical aspect of inevitability. And before you give up the search for answers, you might reminisce and search a little further, this time somewhat vicariously, for traces of redeeming factors. It would do no good to condemn the culture as a whole, but you are dealing with an incident that permeates the culture so deeply it becomes practically unavoidable. You sense a touch of paralysis as you realize the futility of your efforts and you proceed to let it be as that which remains inexplicable, irresolvable, and seemingly irremovable from the basic fabrics of the culture.

But the American culture being what it is, you can always find reason to extricate yourself from a self-imposed mental trap. You shift your mind to something more accommodating, perhaps something more salutary to uplift your spirits. And, of course, there is an abundance of things that would soothe your mind and provide a good measure of instant gratification— in this case, mental. Your latest acquisition might do the trick here or perhaps, the possibility of acquiring a new toy to beef up your collection.

As always, there are countless numbers of diversionary things to take your mind off the very troubling social factor, and this is an essential part of the American culture. The television, depending on the program, to your amazement, or perhaps to your delight, may play the most critical role in this case.

But unfortunately, as you watch some of the programs, you sense the glaring absence of anything cerebral about them. You get the sickening impression of a celebratory preference for the drab, the jejune, and the glaringly nonsensical. You wonder if the intent is to dumb down the society as a whole, or perhaps it is an idea predicated on the assumption that it is a dumb audience for whom such programs are designed to satisfy their low mentality and ultimately soothe their social consciousness in its confines of bovine stupidity. Then, as if the mental assault is not enough, the promotion of a product is surreptitiously stuck in between the programs. The volume is raised to a different decibel. Now you get the impression that the program is not only designed to entertain a fatuous audience but also carefully planned to accommodate the misfortune of their audial deficit.

If the purpose of the programs is to nullify any attempt at serious cerebral activity, then it is a masterful act because the programs not only meet that need but also have the tendency to discourage the inclination for critical thinking. But as in most other things in the society, you still have a choice. You can scan through the programs offered by the various channels to find something more thoughtful and engaging or something else to your liking. As you make such a move, however, you are often reminded by the very nature of the presentation of what you've chosen to watch that the program could be biased in favor of the political or religious sentiments of the presenters. So before you proceed to celebrate a successful escape from the nonsensical and its deplorable ordinariness, you are once again reminded that your choice of program could be tainted by politics and/or the holier-than-thou element of extreme religiosity.

At this point, you may wish to entertain the always helpful advice: buyer beware. Of course, there are programs on television that may be strictly informative and totally free of any political or religious biases, but those are difficult to come by. In some cases, the bias may not be related to anything in your immediate locale or the society at large but related to some other culture that may be cast as a not-so-civilized community. In such instance, the program is packaged as a near mystery from the uncivilized world designed to entertain and whet the appetite of the civilized. Usually, the filming crew and the reporters are seen as daredevil heroes from a civilized environment who not only have the guts to step far into the darkness of these untamed areas but also possess incredibly big hearts. They are seen as godsent, who come with enormous bread baskets including various other magical tidings wrapped in elitist pity and the effusive touch of unctuous humility.

As you watch some of these programs, you are supposed to admire the exceptional heroic undertakings of the civilized crew against the backdrop of a miserably unenlightened group of people whose most salient attribute is a subservient presence marked by ferity and sheepish acquiescence. The coming together of the civilized and the savage becomes an exemplary instance of rescue. The humane touch of the one comes with a terminative blessing to end the suffering of the other and enable him to exuviate his rather ferine inclinations. These programs are designed to entertain you as you wallow in the manifest glory of civilization at its height and savor the luck, which has placed you at a very comfortable distance. At the end of some of these programs, an appealing voice exhorts you to donate kindly toward the continued rescue attempt of these other persons, the improvement of whose fortune could only be possible through your generous contributions.

There are such missions in which people from this society engage in truly humane activities in which they seek to help others in other cultures improve their lives by working with them. But these are often unheralded, and the participants in such activities often prefer the quiet of the absent media and appreciate the sight of the tangible results of their efforts.

So as you sift through the various programs in search of what is truly informative and/or intelligently entertaining, you may hold on to the thought that there could be something on television worth your time and mental application. And like most things in the American culture, there is such an abundance of programs that you can stand a good chance of finding something to your liking.

If you are lucky to find something genuinely appealing, your attempt at mental escape becomes easy, and you cherish this moment because you may find it necessary to seek a mental or even bodily escape from your immediate surroundings more often than you'd wish to do.

As you become very assimilated, you find a good number of things that will uplift your spirits and keep you motivated. But you will also find an equal number, if not more things, that will make you doubt every one of your undertakings. You may even find yourself questioning the validity of your own existence. It is another cultural phenomenon that of necessity becomes inherent as a by-product of a dog-eat-dog social system.

Despite the shortcomings, however, it is still a society capable of offering you so much to choose from along with the tools to help you make the most of your choices.

As a transplant, you will occasionally find yourself in a debate regarding some of the views held by others about your adopted American society. Such debates often become very heated and elicit passionate expressions of some strongly held opinions; and this may set you wondering just why some outside this society entertain negative opinions about your adopted society. With some of these people, you may find it difficult to see any logical reasoning in what they say and continuing to argue with them often leaves you frustrated and disappointed at the fact that neither you nor anyone else could get them to consider other views.

At some other times, you may hear the arguments of some folks who seem to make some rather convincing points about their views. These people may not sound hostile and unwilling to listen to opposing views. They may be accommodating as they invite you to state your views, and they may seem quite willing to think through your points and, by extension, reconsider theirs and explore the possibilities of revisiting the basis of their beliefs; they analyze the implied logic of the constructs and proceed to weigh the merits of its applicability to your point of view.

In either case, however, because this is now your society, you may be inclined to wonder what gives rise to these negative views in the first place. Perhaps it is sheer envy, and perhaps it is lack of understanding. It could be something else that is not readily apparent or succinctly expressed by those detractors of the society. You learn that it is not easy to find adequate reasons to cover all the negatives put forth by these detractors. This is especially true in view of the fact that, in general, the people in this society are essentially nice people who truly demonstrate acts of kindness and the willingness to help others. And, yes, the American culture, like any other human culture, has its own failings; but indeed, the basics of its tenets promote healthy human interactions with tangible results gained from their social application.

So why the very negative views, and why are they expressed with so much anger sometimes? Perhaps everyone agrees that the American society could not be perfect and, most certainly, could not do everything to meet the expectations of everybody, be he/she from this society or another. Even then, as you seek to consider the topic from a point of fairness, you are made aware of some of the things in this society that you'd rather see done differently. Perhaps the issue of ethnicity, including some of the misguided social programs that tend to encourage dependency among some of the people, will stand out. On the other hand, you may want to settle with the thought that it is the nature of the American culture that invites criticism.

The American society is a very dynamic one and, since the essence of societal dynamism implies progressive dialogue, exchange of ideas; and a continuous move from one level of cultural tenet to another, including the frequent birth of one new idea after the other, debates about the culture will always be present. By placing this perspective against a cultural hallmark of openness, unflinching individualism, and uncompromising sense of independence, you have an environment set to encourage and entertain discourse and disagreement.

After witnessing some of the forceful presentations of the views of some detractors of the American culture and its system, you lament the absence of reasoned dialogue and wish for a healthier exchange. But then, you hardly venture very far from your point of departure and you don't really dwell on this issue too long before it hits you: it's a very American thing; it is an aspect of the culture, and the debates you witness are chapters in the practical application of the very essence of freedom. Let's face it, freedom in a society emboldens its citizens and encourages debates among them about their culture.

You may be inclined to wonder, what precisely is your role in all of this? And, of course, you may not be adopting the most admirable posture by believing that you are totally removed from it all and only going along with whatever placates your mind, because like it or not, you are a part of the system and an instrument within the culture and your participation in the daily course of events makes you one of the architects of that for which you are seeking answers. After all, you are present here. Your participation in discussions regarding the merits and demerits of the culture becomes a contributory factor in that process of social dynamism. And in this instance, you are not simply present. You are very present within the system and its cultural trends. In spite of their detraction, the opponents of the culture can also celebrate, particularly when residing in America, what the culture offers them in the name of freedom. Their voices find strength from the knowledge that here's freedom, if not in a true sense, at least from the possibilities evidenced by their ability to voice their opinion without fear of recrimination. The occasion of a debate becomes a process of realizing one of the benefits implied by the statement of freedom. If the detractors were born in America, the debate, for them, becomes a demonstration of their implicit belief in the statement of the culture. If they are foreign residents, it becomes a celebration of that rather unique possibility that necessitated their emigration from their place of birth.

You may find yourself participating in these debates rather too often, particularly if you believe in the American system and feel very strongly about your position or threatened by the appearance of anything seeming to enervate the fundamental principles of a very critical statement of the culture. In such instance, you find yourself playing the role of a dutiful protector. You do this not necessarily because of personal gullibility but in response to the inclination for defending the verism demonstrably present in the letters of the culture. The statement of these letters has a uniqueness of being both explicitly inferent and effectively efferent. In most instances, you find these debates informative, particularly when they are marked by the absence of vindicatory utterances or infelicitous comments couched on unverifiable statements of presumed fact.

As far as debates go, these debates are often exceptionally intense. They arrest your attention even when you are not that interested in participating in them. They also make you think beyond the given. They foster a sense of inquiry that encourages you to seek answers to social issues which you'd otherwise take for granted. In the course of your inquiry, the answers you get may not be totally adequate. Every answer you arrive at may give rise to other questions not apparent to you in the beginning. Since the debate is about your society and its culture

IKE C. UDEH

and the way the culture is perceived by others outside this community, you are inclined to want to find adequate answers to the issues raised because the issues, particularly those that seem valid, may have a direct impact on your daily life. So as you reason through the issues and consider the substance of their import, you lay bare the composition of your mind as you strip it of its cloak of doubt. You also rid your mind of unreasoned credulity and the inclination for stubborn adherence to any one particular view—American or any other.

You may find no answers in the end because such issues often extend beyond a point of finality. They go from one point, back through the same point, in a sort of cyclical extensity, which admits everything in its potential but offers nothing in substance, and that's when you feel drained and spent from the demands of prolonged mental activities.

In America, chances are you will always experience other occasions of a debate on issues of culture, but you ardently wish for one with much less passion and intensity. You hope that, as these detractors of the American system become more socialized into the system, their views will become appropriately modified, perhaps through the process of acculturation. Even after this process, it is still possible to have disagreements about some aspects of the culture. It is necessary that these disagreements exist because they encourage dialogue and ultimately make people think about the culture and about their actions, including how they affect others. It encourages critical thinking in place of a gullible embrace of all the cultural tenets that guide social mores and expectations. And as you assimilate and participate in this dialogue, you find comfort in knowing that you are joining others within the society in advancing the quality of the culture. At the end, as you sift through the lessons learned from each debate, you have much less difficulty realizing what keeps the culture moving and growing, for you've become, through your participation, part of the instrument of change.

CHAPTER VI

Limitations

A S THE SOCIETY proclaims itself the champion of freedom, you may wonder how much of this holds true for you as an individual. You wonder, how far does your freedom extend and to what extent are you truly free? Perhaps the most obvious limitation, which is readily apparent, is the fact that your freedom does not give you the liberty to infringe on others' rights or take actions that may deny their freedom. However, as you analyze this apparent limitation, you realize that it is not so much a limitation as a stopgap designed to protect their freedom and, conversely, yours as well.

As you process the implications of this limitation, you get the nagging feeling there is something within the social structure that appears to limit your freedom. You feel the presence of something societal, which in its manifestation has the potential of undermining your liberty to wallow in the prospects of freedom. There is something inherently limiting within the process of this freedom, and your inquisitive mind is restlessly seeking the culprit element.

Before you find answers to your inquiry, however, you take a moment to appreciate the fact that the very instance of a mental activity, which analytically examines the process of your freedom, is in itself an occasion of freedom. This occasion of personal freedom becomes precisely the incipient instrument in the manifestation of your freedom.

But there are some rather disconcerting instances of limitations, and you are searching for answers.

So what within the social structure appears to diminish your sense of freedom? As a member of the society, and as a true believer in the contents of its dictates, you sincerely hope it is nothing perhaps inadvertently legislated into its letters. But as you continue to hope, you sense the undercurrent of a feeling of discomfort, and this nudges you a few steps beyond the threshold of your current mental endeavors. You begin to search through the repository of your experiences, which include those incidents directed at you and those you witnessed being directed at others. Then you arrive at the issue of ethnic differences, and your mind immediately freezes to a standstill.

Your search has brought you to that ever-present problem within the society and a problem that is fast becoming a constant because of its very frequent occurrence. It is as if, while the society defines ethnicity, ethnicity defines the culture; and this sets the tone and the measure of freedom for the individual.

You've been fortunate to learn from the folks that this is the abode of freedom, and it is yours to embrace and thrive in. You've heard freedom being defined and the process explained in order to enable you and everyone else to enjoy and make the most of it. You are free to move around. You are free to express your opinion. You have freedom of choice. You have the freedom to determine what suits you. You determine what comforts you. And you decide for yourself that course of action that brings you to the realization of your dreams. Oh yes, you can dream, and you are encouraged to dream, and the realization of your dreams is expressly ordained by the accessibility of the contents of your freedom. You figure your existence and its prosperity are guaranteed through the processes of freedom, until you arrive at the factor of ethnicity.

You've arrived at a point where freedom begins to take a variety of definitions, and each definition is determined by ethnicity. At this juncture, your feelings are not exactly irrational and self-serving but based on incidents culled from both personal and observed experiences. You've seen the comportment, the body language, and the posture of the various peoples within the society. You witnessed the distinctions in personal presence. You noticed some people as they emphatically wear their freedom. Their person is garbed in the socially defined outfit of immediate acceptance, and their presence is announced by an obvious air of entitlement. These people often don't have to face the extra courtesy of frequent "Do you need some help?" or "Can I help you?" which make department stores such glorious places.

But you also witnessed the body language of others within the society, and you noticed how their person is marked by a rather subdued presence. You noticed the subtle touch of self-containment and the obvious air of extra caution. In comparison with the former people, it is as if the ethnicity of these people can only guarantee a portion of freedom. These people do not necessarily have to be told what the deal is. They haven't been handed literature that defines freedom differently than the way it is defined for the socially privileged group. But the message is very much there—a message of privileges as defined for each person according to his ethnicity. It is a message that everyone is aware of, and everyone has an opinion according to how it impacts him. Perhaps the message is not exactly legislated into law, but it is deftly accommodated within the social system; and each individual, or institution, has the choice of either exploiting the unfortunate benefits of this message or eschewing its disuniting element of social degradation.

Now you found an answer to a nagging question regarding your freedom. Now the job takes on a different format with different sets of issues. You arrived at the point of ethnicity and how it defines the freedom of the individual in the American society, and because freedom is the one paramount thing that distinguishes the society from others, anything that appears to diminish its privileges and opportunities becomes a critically important item for general consideration. As you deal with the topic of ethnicity, your own ethnic background comes into play; and since the frequency of discrimination according to ethnicity is high, your ethnicity will shape your opinion. As you view yourself through the lenses of your own ethnicity, your opinion becomes shaped by your response to the role ethnicity plays within the social system. Depending on your background, you may even be oblivious to the true impact of this issue on some members of the society and take for granted the extra privileges available to you as an entitlement due to your ethnicity. And this is where some people, in their lamentable ignorance of a very present social stain, begin to step on others' toes, only to follow up with an apology that further rubs in the pain.

If your ethnicity places you in direct contrast with the socially defined criteria for acceptance, your opinion regarding this issue and your responses to the troubling encounters with it will depend on how you've chosen to define the impact of such experiences for yourself. But because your ethnicity can define the extent of your freedom in America, as an individual, your responses to negative incidents of ethnicity may not be enough to guarantee a complete enjoyment of freedom. Yours, then, may be a dichotomous instance of guaranteed freedom with built-in ethnic limitations. How you find your way from this dilemma to the full realization of your freedom becomes an ongoing struggle with a difficult social problem.

As you seek to find your way to the full realization of the freedom, which is supposedly guaranteed to you and everyone else in America, you become quite conscious of your person within and outside your immediate environment. You do not necessarily wear the look of despondence or interact with others from a defeatist standpoint. You don't try to play ignorant and come off as if you're OK with the thought that your kind have been socially ordained to play the second fiddle among the others. You do not have to force the issues or want to let others dictate the terms of your participation as if in an attempt to appease and appeal for acceptance through the silence of your acquiescent presence. You simply play from the standpoint of fairness, firmness, and implicit belief that it is a ball game designed by humanity, for humanity for the ultimate realization of truly amicable human interaction, as a guarantee for humanity's own peaceful existence.

Perhaps the more difficult task you may have to deal with in America is how to explain to a prospective immigrant the impact of ethnicity on the all-important factor of freedom, which defines the American society. If the topic concerns those factors that are natural constraints within freedom, the job is practically self-done; and one of these could be that aspect of freedom that demands a sense of restraint from the individual. You'd be hard-pressed, however, to find adequate explanations for why an individual's ethnicity can determine the limits of the freedom the society accords him.

You may not find the most adequate answers to your questions, but you will feel some sense of gratification from the exercise, because by setting your mind on this rather troubling social issue, you begin to explore the possibilities of either transcending it or helping to bring about some changes.

In the end, as you exit from the quandary, you may find yourself freshly armed with some extra knowledge that may guide you toward a more rewarding sense of freedom. You find yourself engaging and participating with confidence and a firm sense of purpose. You are now more focused on your goals because what you've done is to precisely transcend the constraints of a social stain; and by your action, you avoided the blame game and worked within yourself to find answers, which may not only help you but also has the potential of contributing toward the improvement of the system as a whole. After all, the American society has a way of always reminding you that you are an intrinsic part of it. The elegance of the beauty of the society is a function of your reasoned contribution, and the ultimate realization of its betterment is guaranteed by the individual's appreciation of its failings and his determination to work toward the processes of change.

The establishment of a society such as the American, the hallmark of which is freedom for its citizens, denotes a noble process of governance, which provides the opportunity for the individual to work toward the realization of his goals. In turn, this process promises the continued advancement of the society as a whole. Especially in the American society, the right of freedom also embodies the freedom of spirit designed to encourage free thinking without constraints due to your person, your beliefs, etc. But since your person is an embodiment of your ethnicity, social incidents that adversely affect your person become a limitation of your freedom. Though there are programs ostensibly designed to prevent the infringement of the individual's freedom, some of these programs are either inadequate or poorly administered. In some instances, it is as if the programs themselves create the opportunity for anyone with the motive to take actions that limit another's freedom.

Often, those people whose freedom is adversely constrained because of their ethnicity will express their feelings regarding the impact such constraint has on them.

According to these people, it isn't so much the practical experience of such constraints as the mental experience that does the most harm. This experience has the ability to limit the victim's potential by undermining his drive and the desire to work toward the realization of his dreams. The person is thus stripped of the spiritual energy, which sustains his efforts. He is subsequently left with a mentality predisposed to giving up at the dawn of any obstacle, particularly that which appears to have a correlation to his ethnicity. This person ultimately becomes a victim of a dehumanizing social occurrence, which then marks him with the label of failure, which further drives him toward the bottom of the social ladder. It becomes awfully difficult and often impossible for these folks to dig themselves out of this social situation of mental internment.

IKE C. UDEH

This situation in America, the victims will tell you, creates a deplorable mental condition in which the person hears freedom and sees freedom; and all around him, he witnesses others enjoying the full benefits of freedom. He is told he is totally free like most of the people; and, of course, the society encourages him to dream like most of the people. But he realizes that for him, the full enjoyment of freedom is only possible within the very private and silent confines of his mind. His, then, becomes a unique instance of measured freedom—the design and extent of measurement socially determined according to his ethnicity.

Are these persons really free?

Some people will state that the idea of freedom is relative. Some would say it is encapsulated within the mind of the individual. Yet others would insist that victim or no victim, everyone is free in America and that these so-called victims need only compare their situation to that of those people who live in a society governed by a dictator.

But those people whose freedom has been curtailed, in addition to having their mental scars to show for it, will point to the fact that these folks who downplay and dismiss their plight are from the socially privileged group. They are nonvictims, who would cite irrelevant situations to support their claims and minimize the potential of a guilt feeling.

As a newly settled citizen in America, your reaction to the remarks of those people who have not had the misfortune of suffering discrimination according to their ethnicity will depend on your ethnicity, including the circumstances in which you experience those remarks. But there is nearly always something you cannot avoid, and that is the fact that you will run into people who will make such remarks sometimes as often as they see fit. Such insensitive remarks are sometimes used by some people to gain a mental advantage over their victim.

These remarks may not necessarily foster a deep-seated regret within you or make you view the whole American social system as irredeemably hostile. It will, however, open your eyes to some of the social incidents that you would not be aware of otherwise. Primarily, it will alert you to the fact that though it is a pluralistic society with a melting-pot facade, it is essentially divided according to the individual's ethnic background. There is also the social division according to wealth and money, and when you add these two factors to the issue of ethnicity, you have a society that is inherently fractionalized and having difficulty truly putting into practice some of its excellent ideals.

But as you go about your daily business in America—and this is mainly for your own sanity—you proceed with a positive mind-set and the best intentions. This approach, in addition to its healthy appeal, encourages your inclination to contribute to the social changes that may improve the society as a whole. In some cases, however, your experience with a negative social incident may be frustrating enough to make you suspect that some of those people who consciously choose to discriminate against you, particularly in a rather hostile manner, will only cease such actions after a pointed hostile response from you. No doubt, you will encounter people like these, but you have to decide for yourself if it's worth anything for you to stoop to their level. And this is when you choose magnanimity over solicited hostility. But you still need to be mindful of the fact that, in American society, being magnanimous is sometimes perceived as a sign of weakness; and as a victim of such perception, you are more likely to be victimized again by the same people. In time, as a newly settled person, you learn that yours is a society that has no tolerance for weakness.

Such misguided perception of weakness is not a cultural trait that is difficult to grasp. It is not one that is intolerable either because, in time, you will find room in your mind to not only accommodate it but also exhibit such traits when you feel it is necessary. One of the remarkable things about the American society is that, as you assimilate, you adopt most of the cultural traits, including some of those ones that you did not quite approve of initially. Some of the newly settled folks would say this is because it behooves you to adopt as many of the practices as possible. That way, you make it easier for yourself to blend. Yet others would claim that this is another example of the seductiveness of the culture, which promises true freedom for the individual, only to make it truly possible according to his ethnicity. It may be difficult to accept the latter argument, particularly since as an individual you do have choices; and yes, it is not that easy to resist this seductiveness. But being aware of it strengthens your ability to make a more reasonable choice.

As you struggle with the issue of ethnicity and how it impacts yours and others' freedom in America, you may be inclined to consider how you view yourself within the society. Your self-perception may be shaped not only by your own view of yourself but also by the way the society impacts you. All this, in turn, may determine how you relate to others in your society; it may also shape the nature of your expectations from the society. Underlying the self-perception and your expectations are the traits you learned from your previous culture, and this is especially true if you had arrived in America with a preformed sense of right and wrong. And in some cases, depending on where you hailed from, such undercurrent of preexisting acculturation could prove to be constraints that may limit your capability to realize all the benefits offered by the freedom in your new society.

Of course, such personal constraints do not necessarily negate the role ethnicity plays in the American society, but it invariably makes a negative experience because of ethnicity worse. You become hypersensitive. But if you are lucky enough to have hailed from a situation from which you developed a strong sense of self and a rather positive outlook on life, you may be able to transcend some of those negative social incidents of ethnicity in America. And for those incidents that seem difficult to transcend, you may find that these are still very unpleasant things to deal with. In this your new society, the idea of freedom plays an interesting role in the everyday life of the individual, and every/anything that affects a person's freedom, especially if it is negative, has a profound impact on the person's life.

On occasion, you wonder if there is anything about the issue of ethnicity in America that offers something positive and worth entertaining as a worthy social instrument for amicable coexistence. You may also wonder if your ethnic background is truly the one very obvious trait, which immediately defines your person within any social context. Your search could leave you pondering over the criteria utilized to define the various persons who make up the general population in America. You may be tempted to reevaluate these criteria and search for their origin, which apparently came from the customs and practices of one particular culture; and essentially, these customs and practices are mostly Western.

It's been a while since you left one society for the American. You are beginning to feel quite assimilated, and you structure your life and daily activities according to the norms of the society. Your activities, including preoccupations and inclinations, begin to fall in line with the cultural tenets you're beginning to accept. But you experience some discomforts, which often arise from some of the doubts you entertain. You feel rather inclined to extricate these doubts from the contents of your critical mind in order to focus your whole attention on the more appealing aspects of the culture. But you find your efforts undermined by the very process of this mental exercise, perhaps because the criteria you employ are culled from the norms defined as acceptable by the same social system you find troubling. Now you begin to sense the rather distasteful experience of being at a no-win situation. You wonder for a moment if you are being too critical of those aspects of the culture which do not sit too well with you. After all, every culture has its negative attributes and the American is no different.

Apparently, what has plagued you for a while now is the role ethnicity plays in the society. Ethnicity has, therefore, become that part of the American social system that you and most of the others around you would like to redefine and ultimately place in what may be considered a much more generally accepted perspective. The redefinition you feel would be best, of course, would be that which would accommodate the varying preferences of the different peoples of this pluralistic society. This may seem daunting and rendered impossible by the expediency of the exercise. And since ethnicity is a constant that plays in every facet of social interaction, there emerges a necessity underscored by its pressing immediacy.

And as you wrestle with what appears to be an irresolvable problem, the traveler wonders just how far off your goal this exercise might take you. He lets this issue play and replay itself within his mind. It often seems as if some of these topics are playing by and of themselves with no direct or active input from the traveler.

But it is this rather constant statement that hovers or, rather, drifts within the confines of his mind that appears to mitigate or bolster the impact of this and other seemingly vexing topics:

> There is a being in every traveler
> And a traveler in every being

You are tempted to shy away from this seemingly impossible task, and you may feel that any attempt at changing things would be a waste of time. But you can hardly stay away from the issue of ethnicity in America, and you simply cannot discountenance the role it plays socially, including the seriousness of its very negative impact on practically every social interaction.

IKE C. UDEH

The more difficult aspect of your dilemma may be the nagging thought that, even as you seek to find more tolerable ways of employing ethnicity in social interactions, there is something regarding ethnicity within your reach. You are aware that sometime in the not-so-distant past, somewhere within your immediate environment, or somewhere in your path and steeped in the confines of your daily activities, there is something rather insalubrious that is predicated on ethnicity. And with such realization, it feels as if you are always confronted by issues of ethnicity in practically every aspect of your life.

You suspect this is a problem shared by all, but you still remain aware that the way ethnicity plays out socially in the American society, the effect of the impact is differently experienced by the victim and the player. Since the urgency of redefining the factors that appear to lend credence to social norms is increased according to your own personal experience, you search for answers for yourself. You might even find answers through a seemingly innocuous process. So you invariably fall back to the very fundamental element of the American social system— it is that which guarantees you and others the inalienable right to existence.

In the ultimate, you may find your mind buoyed by the rather elegant aspects of the American culture and your presence anchored by the basic letters of the system. It is democratic. It is free. And the process of governance is predicated on the importance of the individual as an intrinsic part of the whole. Of course not, you haven't quite transcended the problematic issue of ethnicity. But apparently, you've found a launching pad, a point of departure that propels you to the next thought process. In this process, you borrow the very letters of the system and their obvious implication that seeks to offer you and others the actuality of everything they promise. Thus, the system aims to shy away from mere pretenses, which would otherwise suggest an instance of dancing at the outskirts of freedom and flirting with the nuances of democratic governance.

Perhaps, in accord with your mental exercise, what eventuated is that the criteria used to determine the norms in your new society are not exactly blessed with sacrosanctity and universality; these norms are borrowed from the customs and practices of a particular ethnic group—that being the Western.

So you seek comfort and reassurance from the inner recesses of your being. You tap into the reservoir of some rather personal convictions anchored by experience and guaranteed to sustain you in times of doubt and social discomfort. You may not see yourself being able to solve such a problematic social issue as ethnicity, which is disconcerting in its misuse and divisive in its practical application as the sole determinant in critical decisions affecting the greater generality of the people. And you may feel impotent and essentially destined to live with the unpleasantness of the apparent societal insensitivity to the issue. But you hold on to your conviction nonetheless, for this is what precisely buoys your spirit and keeps you going.

Perhaps you admired those instances of apparent magnanimity by that politician who frequently hollered and made far-reaching promises of social change— changes that are designed to rid the American society of its insensitivity to the misuse of ethnicity in both private and social contexts. The words of this politician were so convincing and the potential of the ultimate application of the promise so encouraging that you felt there was cause for hope for a meaningful social change. But something within you suggested caution, particularly since you have heard such promises come and go. Perhaps you can hardly forget instances in which such promises were ceremoniously *signed* into place, ostensibly as a form of incrementalism that would ultimately bring about a social change. So you tone down the apparent joy and effectively curb your enthusiasm. And in the end, your rather cautious sense of judgment prevails. Your incredulity is lent credence as the passage of time sees no change in the status quo.

Of course, you do not exactly fault the big-mouth politician, for he/she is quick to suggest that the essence of the promise is rendered inextensible because of insurmountable obstacles within the social structure. In a word, this person is saying that the promise of change was made in good faith, but it was not possible to extend the benefits therein to everyone in the community; and in addition, the opponents in the other party scuttled the plans. The subtext here, you may notice, is "Vote for me next time around, for I really promise, this time, to do battle with those bastards."

At this juncture, does the trend of events presage a depletion in spirit, and is it truly a no-win situation?

And that is a question you and others around you are beginning to view as essentially rhetorical. You sense a deterioration within the social structure. You grapple with the very evident instance of social malaise, which is underscored by an apparent preference for insouciance. You see no promising signs of meaningful social change, and at times, you suspect a stagnation in the progressive essentials of the social system; and this, you suspect, becomes the incipient signs of societal retrogression.

And the traveler wonders!

Social retrogression? Perhaps a more palatable situation would be progress rather than regress; and this appears to take on an added life of its own as the traveler considers how much effort a community of humans invests in its efforts to keep its society from regressing.

But you are rather hesitant to make an absolute condemnation of one social system as opposed to another. You know only too well that all social systems have that inherent quality that positively affirms their human design and, as such, makes them less than perfect.

Then, you are left with the odd but well-grounded feeling that whether in America or elsewhere, the various social systems are all instances of manmade structures that make up a stage. And on this stage, the actors are the audience and the audience, the actors. The drama is constituted of their activities. As the drama proceeds, they all remain aware of the futility of their actions. But being humans, it is just fine with them because they will themselves into pretenses and permanently live in pretenses because they've codified the essence of pretense into a seemingly meaningful manner of existence. In the ultimate, the evident predilection notwithstanding, humans all strut to the clumsy trill of an unfortunate music that, perchance, will numb their senses and ameliorate the preordained realities of their existence.

And this is the very circumstance of the human course you thought you'd escaped when you left your society of birth for America.

And now you know, there is no paradise!

Perhaps you can create a feeling of paradise in your mind and try to let that translate into the guiding principle of your everyday life. This way, you might be closer to a scenario you thought was existent in the American society before you arrived. But as you seek to create your own perfectly blissful society, you may be nudging yourself toward living in isolation, essentially mentally. And since it is practically impossible for the individual to live in isolation in America while participating in the activities around him, your endeavor becomes a particularly daunting and literally impossible task.

As the resident people in America will tell you, yours may not be an entirely unique case of mental isolation, and most certainly, you are not alone in this life choice of a physical presence wrapped in a mindset of mental absence. And if you are lucky enough, you will soon run into others in the society who have chosen to live a lifestyle similar to the one you are seeking to adopt. Such an encounter would leave its mark on you because you can't help but notice the weirdness about these persons. And you may not find their presence very appealing as this is marked by a gait that suggests a pitiful disconnection between the person and his environment.

But this is America. Your chosen lifestyle still remains your own personal affair, and how you carry on, particularly in relation to the life circumstances around you, is essentially your business. Whether you choose to live in mental isolation may not really be of concern to your neighbor, and your rather unorthodox lifestyle may be regarded as yet another phenomenon in human existence.

In the end, if you are very settled in this system of living and convinced about its utility to your being, you may not need to worry about how it plays out on the social scene. As long as it suits you and nurtures the essence of your existence, you are quite OK. For this, too, is expressly guaranteed equal protection by the American system.

And, yes, that's another element of beauty in the American culture. There is ample room for all, including the great, the pious, the extrovert, and his social opposite and, also, the social misfit and the socially misguided. And there is room for those folks who have chosen a life in isolation, including those whose physical presence remains partially empty and only functioning with a transient mind and a set of diminished faculties.

But before you hop on a soapbox to translate this broad room for all into a negative aspect of the American system, you may want to think beyond these borders and remember some of the sanctioned practices in some of those other societies. Some of these practices are not exactly very admirable, and chances are that was one of the primary motivating factors that encouraged your relocation.

And quite rightly, apparently, the traveler's thoughts dip into this stretch of varying probabilities one of which could be applicable to your

IKE C. UDEH

situation. If you emigrated from one of those societies with an oppressive social system, then your chosen American society becomes both the result and a function of a rather brilliant move. But, he surmises, perhaps in keeping with the mind-set of being in every traveler, your move was not simply brilliant but also an instance of rescue and in this instance, the traveler admits, a rescue for the being.

It could be that the system you left behind in your previous society, in your view, has so much to offer and can boast a well-balanced system in which everyone is equally protected and everyone enjoys the same measure of opportunities and privileges. And perhaps you have reason to believe that in your old society people are not as judgmental as in the American society. But you'd be hard-pressed to find a society in which its citizens are all truly on equal level socially. Even those societies that claim to function on a system without any class consciousness still have a certain measure of social classification—a sort of hierarchical placement of its people that is often based on wealth, family connections, and/or political clout. And any advantages in such classifications are often socially important and sought after.

In the American society, you may at times find it difficult to grasp the disconnect between what the system preaches and promises and what actually plays out in practice. You may even feel disillusioned by the inadequacy of the system when it comes to the question of being innocent until proven guilty. This rather admirable principle offers an exceedingly exemplary element that promises to make the system a truly functional material designed to cater to the wellbeing of its citizens. It is implicit in this principle that the system is for the people and not the other way around. Depending on the circumstance of the situation in which you find yourself, however, your person plays a very important role; and this could be the factor that reverses the principle, thus leaving you guilty before you are even tried. And like it or not, your gender sometimes plays a significant role in the application of this principle.

Perhaps this is where some conservatives in American politics have a lot more to offer than any other social faction. It often seems it is the conservatives who would often question why it appears that, as a male, the system may be more readily inclined to find ample reasons for which you are guilty even before you offer any statements in your own defense. It is as if being male automatically predisposes you to being guilty in most situations while the element of femininity immediately precludes sociopathic tendencies and criminal inclinations.

And as it often seems, being male in America, you are more vulnerable to social condemnation. And it is not uncommon for some people of the male species to feel so persecuted that they begin to act out their frustrations. But this becomes counterproductive since acting out does not necessarily begin to address the issue. At this point, if you are male, you may want to find some consolation in the fact that, in the end, the system often comes around in the process of offering a more balanced approach to the treatment of both sexes.

If you are so caught up in a totally negative view of the system that it becomes impossible for you to find any redeeming value in it, you may be missing out on some of the benefits that might otherwise be right at your doorstep. As in any human society, the beauty in the American system makes itself apparent and available when the negative factors are balanced against the good. You may even want to remind yourself that, directly or indirectly, you are a contributing subject to both the good and the not-so-great aspects of the system. Essentially, you are one of the architects of the system. The fact that you've chosen to busy yourself with interminable criticism while pretending to sit on the fence does not really make you an innocent bystander. Let's face it, being a sitter on the fence suggests an idle opportunist, who's ready to take and enjoy whatever good the system presents while not having anything to offer.

As a transplant in America, you may run into those people who would always argue with you in the process of trying to convince you about how bad the system is. Such people are not necessarily bad people or unpatriotic people. Often, you'll find that these are some of the most decent people, pretty well informed, but a little off the mark in their relentless pursuit of an impossible utopia. In most instances, these folks make a very good point, and you'll find that the system as a whole could use some of their ideas. But it is often their insistence on holding on to an absolutist approach that leaves you searching for the factors that might serve as redemptive elements for these otherwise decent souls.

An interesting thing about the presence of these folks is that they too are very welcome and comfortably accommodated by the system.

IKE C. UDEH

But this is your now-adopted society, and there is something about its culture that attracted you in the first place and motivated you to relocate. And this is meant to be the ultimate in a human attempt at creating a perfect scene for human habitation. It is a theater of sorts, designed for substance, built on substance, and supposedly detailed in substance. There was a point of inception when it all got started, there was a midpoint when the undertaking seemed impossible to accomplish, and there was that period when the endeavor became possible and the fruits of the human labor became apparent and tangible. And this period of the manifestation of the essence of the dream became a realization that is evidenced by this moment of social beneficence that promises to reach every aspect of the American system.

As a transplant, the more you wade into the rather intricate designs that form the foundations of the America system, the more you are inclined to lose yourself in the complexities of this human undertaking. And often, as you begin to grasp the intricacies therein, the system appears to lend itself to whatever interpretation you might be inclined to give its fundamental attributes. You are tempted to let your thoughts dwell on the possibilities that might lay ahead and wonder what could be the case if situations change. After all, no condition is permanent, and this truism applies to all human activities. You weigh this prospect and consider its potentials by letting your mind sift through the annals of history and flirt with relevant historical antecedents. Every civilization ultimately falls. Every fall marks the beginning of another. The beginning often presages a period of doubt and uncertainty. You shudder momentarily as you try to recoil from the disconcerting impact of this mental exercise. The American system may not really be perfect but—

So you let these fleeting moments of query sail through and out of your mind and ultimately drift into the quiet of their absence, for there is something silently disquieting about them. Perhaps you end up viewing this mental journey as a period of unquiet interlude in the daily grind of mental exercises. And perhaps you view it all as a necessary exercise, the vitality of which is a poignant reminder that nothing human lasts forever or is perfect. But at the plenitude of such mental exercise, a barely audible voice from its distance in a corner of your being appears to affirm an all-too-human experience as it whispers:

It is a human process;
There are no guarantees,
There are no absolutes;

It is a fading moment,
The empirical evidence,
Of all transient beings;

And this, is a dance,
Terminal, and finite,
Only sustained through pretense.

Again, the traveler opts for silence, preferring to let the moments explain themselves. Perhaps this whole experience is different than you've imagined all along; this is not exactly what you thought, and these experiences of yours are not really existent, essentially not in any human sphere. You are alone in a void; there is nothing human or made by humans around. These circumstances are only playing themselves into your mind; your mind is not actively grasping them but being laden with moments of seeming occurrences and capturing yourself and the essence of your being. It is, perhaps, an instance beyond a being and occurrences beyond explanation. You are the object; your being is being drawn into this void that does not quite hold you captive but disables the process through which your mind can actively and consciously participate. Perhaps it is no mystery, but if it deals in the abstract, plays in a void—an emptiness that has *nothing* for its substance, then your mind is being forced to toil in its own nonexistence. Perhaps you may not be able to stop the process, you may not be able to extricate your mind from the grasp of these occurrences, but it continues.

And you?
Your being?
Your mind?

As it is, in the ultimate (if time really applies), the entirety of it all may play as the abstract instances of *nothing*. And your being may not truly be; but it all goes on, and on beyond whatever a mind could attempt to perceive within emptiness and into the confines of absolute nothingness.

It proceeds.
And yourself?

You are simply the object of nonhuman occurrences, played out in the abstract void of nothingness. But you proceed— better yet, you think you proceed—the process within is imagined. But you remain captive and only nudged by the void and sounds that play to the moment but beyond your mind's grasp.

Perhaps you hear something!
And perhaps there is nothing audible;
You may want to hold tight on to whatever reaches your grasp.
This, perhaps, is the deep end of void.

But something about your being, something perhaps indefinable, is or rather obtains somewhere; and perhaps for want of logical explanation, or simply for comfort, all instances might presuppose you or simply the essence of your being obtains in America.

CHAPTER VII

Working with the System

A S YOU CONSIDER the system in America and its intricate designs, the topic you had been working on—ethnicity—becomes more significant and an increasingly difficult issue. In such a complex social system, which demands every bit of your mental effort, the misapplication of ethnicity in most social interactions becomes a very disturbing factor of social inequity.

For a transplant, there may be a small advantage in dealing with this issue. The fact that you were not born here offers a slightly more comfortable mental approach than one who was born here. For a start, your perspective on most social issues may have been shaped by a cultural upbringing, which defines social situations and interactions differently than the American system. You will still feel the unsavory impact from the misapplication of ethnicity in the system, but the severity of this impact may be mitigated by extenuating factors culled from this difference in cultural foundations. It is as if somewhere in the confines of your subconscious thoughts there is a mental ability to fall back to this other system from the old culture. This may only be a mental activity engaged in for sheer mental comfort; but nonetheless, it provides a slight insulation and ultimately a measure of confidence.

And there are no mysteries.

What you gain from this situation may not effectively shield you from the discomfort that follows after you've experienced discrimination or an insult that has racial bias at its core. It is only that your response to the situation may be somewhat different than it would be from a native. This instance becomes more evident if your ethnic background places you in the minority, particularly if you are black. This may be easier to see from the fact that being a foreign-born black in America you have different cultural experiences that shape your views and often determine how you respond to most social situations and incidents. As a foreign-born black in America, you may lack the history and the ethnic culture that have several generations of persons and decades of social injustice for points of reference.

It may be easy for you to jump to conclusions and make condemnations when you encounter a native-born black who complains about an incident of racial discrimination. And as a transplant, you may hear such complaints quite often. They may even begin to seem like unnecessary complaints that provide no benefit to anyone. But this feeling may be because you cannot truly relate to the historical basis of such complaints. Granted, there are occasions when the complainer appears to be more inclined to dwell permanently on this issue, and such is the case when the person begins to strike you as refusing to march forward and seems unwilling to utilize the past injustice as a motivating springboard for self-improvement and advancement. But even in a situation such as this, it might be more prudent to be less critical because you just might not know what circumstances both personal and social are impinging upon the individual's senses.

And yet, there are no mysteries.

Still in a quandary?

The mind may struggle as the instance of nonbeing waddles in its attempts to present a form.

And the traveler?

As you struggle with the issue of ethnicity, including other vexing issues in the American system, you may wonder if it is at all possible to change those aspects of the system that create room for the misuse of these issues, particularly when the issues are employed to foster an instance of discrimination or persecution. With respect to ethnicity, since you are aware of the fact that this, in and of itself, is not a bad component within any population of people, your search for possible changes then is focused on those social practices in which the application of ethnicity determines the measure of freedom and, ultimately, the well-being of the individual. And in those cases in which this practice appears to have been institutionalized either by design or by omission, the idea of fostering a change becomes a daunting task. Sometimes the task is not only daunting but practically impossible.

You feel that your efforts are challenged at every step; you even experience overt hostility and/or violence being directed at you. Now you find yourself not only wrestling with the misapplication of ethnicity but also having to worry about your physical safety.

For some, this becomes a point at which a retrospective look at their efforts, which they considered magnanimous, begins to erode their confidence and belief in the American system. Some may even begin to question their judgment and the soundness therein, particularly since they've always believed the system to be that in which their persons are respected and accepted as equal. But if you find yourself willing and able to proceed with your efforts at encouraging a change, you may begin to suspect that in dealing with the topic of institutionalized discrimination and the like in America, the enemy is not necessarily the system but, essentially, your neighbor.

Like everyone else within the society, experience tells you that every aspect of the system is brought into practical manifestation by the people who comprise the society. And chances are, you have personal experiences that need nothing else to substantiate your suspicion that that fellow person, who often professed sincerity and good neighborliness, just might be the very opposite. Your sense of curiosity, coupled with a sense of fairness, now eggs you on. You wonder about those times in which you'd interacted with such persons. You also wonder how many times you've mistaken such persons for what you thought they were, and that could make you shudder at what may appear to make you seem gullible.

Since you believe your efforts to be genuine, you may be able to proceed with a stronger determination because you can then remind yourself that your goal is to encourage the search for a change in the system. You may be encouraged by the knowledge that that person whose deplorable behavior was a regrettable experience for you quite possibly didn't have much to offer in the name of personal goodness or social decency. In such instance, this is a person who has unfortunately lowered his humanity to the point that he/she seeks to compensate for such lamentable misdeeds through personal aggrandizement. In any given social situation, ethnocentric utterances become the substance of this person's discourse.

Your primary mission, however, is not exactly spending time to educate every one of such persons who comes your way. Nor are you

IKE C. UDEH

about to let such encounters alter your direction. If anything, such could be an occasion that helps you stay focused on a goal that may promote a change in the system. The difficulty in your mission then becomes dealing with the question: "Is this possible?" It may not matter if this is your society of birth or you are transplanted from a different one. You are seeking an affirmative answer to this question. And you are dealing with a human society. You are talking humanity, of which you are a part.

If you, by any chance, feel that it is possible to change the unsavory aspect of the system, then your next task is to find the most effective process.

As you proceed, several ideas may drop into your mind and you could perhaps let yourself wallow in the apparent abundance of the possibilities and the seeming quickness at which your efforts bore fruits after an initial search through a rather brief sedulous investigation.

You can consider the various processes you could possibly utilize. You may be inclined to start by having some conversations with your various neighbors. In this case, some of the very people you may be talking with could be some of those same persons who epitomize those social blemishes you are trying to change. The good thing about this could be the fact that you may not have to do much work or travel too far to find your subjects.

With this process, your preparations will include several personal attributes that will include a rather thick skin and the ability to disregard some of the threats that may be designed to discourage you, provoke you, or simply spell out in your face the futility of your mission as they see it.

There may be other discouraging incidents as you proceed, and some of them could be akin to the violent type. But you can choose to remain steadfast. After all, you are quite prepared for this; as it is said he who eats with the devil must have a long spoon. So you are prepared to have your discussion, albeit a rather difficult one but, hopefully, ultimately a fruitful one. And, of course, your efforts are predicated on the firm belief that through a process of reasoned, accommodating, and intelligent discourse, an amicable process of coexistence can be achieved.

Depending on how your discussions turn out, this could be an undertaking you may have to stay with for a long time, particularly since the very nature of the American society is such that it seems incapable of defining itself without the issue of ethnicity. You get the unsettling feeling that your efforts will always be marred by the overriding threat of ethnicity that seems so deeply entrenched in every aspect of the system as to be practically irreversible. And then you really wonder if any change is possible. You may then be inclined to find an explanation for this dilemma and proceed to look at the American society from a broader perspective. And one possible explanation could be that, since every society has its own blemishes, the misuse of ethnicity in your adopted American society is one of its own failings.

This explanation, however, may leave you with that same unsettling feeling that could be very difficult to eradicate. You may also have to live with this dilemma because at every corner, in whatever context, your new society tells you that the American system is not simply the best social system there is but also the one and only example by which others should structure themselves. It is such outright condemnation of other societies that appears to nullify any explanation you may try to offer, especially since your new society often leaves no room for a possible redefinition of what a much more balanced social system should be. And according to some detractors, it is a very American cultural attribute to condemn other social systems while offering unrealistic ideas, wrapped in Yankee idealism and sold on the platform of its unique impracticality.

But this is America, your new society. You've transplanted yourself, or you have been transplanted. You are a part of it, an intrinsic part to boot. And by your continued presence, you invariably lend credence to the proclamations of the system. Your participation, private or public, substantiates the very principles on which the system rides. You may choose, perhaps for personal comfort, to adopt a dissociative position and pretend to wear the right of the social critic whose sworn endeavor is to always point out every aspect of the system that departs from the perfect. And you may feel quite comfortable in this role, especially since the attendant feeling of exaltation appears to initiate a latent sense of mental gratification. But try telling your story, along with the attempt at dissociation, to a detractor from outside the American system!

Your search, therefore, continues as you look for ways to live with that aspect of the social system that leaves you wondering if it all could

IKE C. UDEH

have been better framed to accommodate and better utilize the natural variety that adorns the presence of every individual.

And as you watch the neighbors play their role—and these are some of those same folks with whom you had your discussion on ethnicity—you notice the distinctions in operation. And this is quite heartening as it immediately suggests an essential attribute of freedom. You witness each person doing his own thing, each one responding to the silent tune of an internal music that only plays to his own personal hearing. You may be lulled into a somewhat soothing mental disposition, encouraged by the thought that this is the practical application of the phrase "to each his own." But as you take in the various activities and sift through the varied impacts of their actions, you begin to sense that "to each his own" may not exactly be such a totally desirable component of social interaction. And that could be because experience may have told you that what "his own" entails may not necessarily be to your own well-being.

As you witness the various activities of each person around you, you experience and appreciate that which truly plays as honestly personal and designed to simply pass you by with consideration for you and others. But you may have difficulty dealing with those negative activities that seem to gain strength from their apparent institutionalization. So even as you seek to entertain the benefits of that which is socially admirable, you find your otherwise pleasant experience is tinged with an accompaniment of the socially indecent.

So did you find a solution? Perhaps you feel you are pretty close but not quite at the threshold of a possible tool for change.

That brings you to the doorstep of your next quandary, which becomes how to utilize any tools you've chanced upon and precisely how your actions could impact the system, if at all.

It begins to seem, at this point, that your efforts have become the offspring of a perennial undertaking, particularly since any workable change has to be broadly accommodating. It not only has to accommodate the varying degrees of individual perceptions that are often sustained by a particular cultural tenet but also sustain its vitality through its social applicability. You realize every individual in America hails from a particular subgroup with its own culture and inclinations. But like you, they all live and interact within the bounds of this society and its system; and despite the background of some ethnic differences, they are all united by a singular thread of national identity. This national identity is further cemented by language.

As a transplanted resident in America whose assimilation is constantly in progress, you notice some changes in the system that are designed to accommodate some of the new residents. You witness some of the newer residents as they initiate some very heated debates and watch some of these changes put in place, not necessarily because of the convincing arguments of the proponents or the overriding benefice of their utility. You suspect that some of these social changes were put in place to satiate the apparent anger of some and quiet the hollering that has vehemence and disquiet for its essential means of communication. As you travel through the various communities, you may witness a multitude of signs, in various forms of communication, all telling the same story. So in place of one simple sign in one medium doing the job of effectively informing the public, you are faced with a clutter of messages, some of them requiring a contortion of your neck and the immediate transformation of your brain in the process of trying to read the words. In the end, you don't exactly read the words but fervently hope it's all a direct translation of the English version, which would have been just fine by itself.

So now, as you wonder why the clutter, you seek to remain positive in consideration for others. You begin to endow these rather exotic foreign language messages with an artistic presence. But as you exit the scene, you wear a smile so you don't let a look of disgust betray your sentiments. But goodness knows, something about these multiple signs in various media begs for further review. And as you grapple with this experience, you struggle to silence a tiny voice and the temptation that tells you the whole darn place is on a backward order.

Well, at this juncture, you may be tempted to wonder if there is truly beauty in variety.

But before you get carried away by the constrained thinking of narrow-mindedness and the limitations of personal sentiments, you are invariably encouraged by nature itself to appreciate the overwhelming evidence of the inherent beauty in variety. After all, the sheer monotony and the repetitious dullness of sameness may make the prospects or the lack of variety downright sickening.

Okay, so you haven't been able to find a workable solution to some of the more vexing social issues in America, but your experience from some of the signs placed around to inform you and others alike leaves more to be desired. As a responsible resident who feels a part of the system, your search for changes to some of the aspects of the social system may be predicated not simply on the willingness to contribute to the positive processes of change but also on the instinct for meaningful and comfortable existence. You may be inclined, therefore, to redouble your efforts at the appearance of seemingly insurmountable obstacles. Perhaps you are now convinced that there is no need for a multitude of signs in various media all telling the same story. After all, a sense of fairness tells you that such changes, by extension, discriminate against others in the community whose primary medium of communication is not represented. You begin to wonder if the solution to this is to let the one main medium of communication stand. Besides, why the pretense when literally everything else, including the sum total of everyone's earnings, is in English?

Of course, it is necessary to recognize the importance and value of the other languages besides English. This may be done, particularly in private matters, by making sure the recipients of information understand what's being communicated to them.

Being a transplanted resident in America, like the resident people, you are pretty OK—at least until the word *dollar* begins to show up in some slightly unreadable language. Then you may really be in trouble because even the letters IRS would have taken a different form, and God help you if you fail to respond when they need to hear from you. Oh yes, you'll be dead—indeed, very dead—before you know what hit you!

As you proceed with your endeavor, it is likely that you'll touch on practically everything within the message of the American system. You will, in the process, arrive at the point at which you may want to apply the Constitution and its contents to some of these difficult social issues.

At first glance, this may seem like the end of your search and the overall solution to your social problems. This may be because you are dealing with the Constitution. And this is a very heavy word pregnant with various tidings and loaded with far-reaching implications. You've come to understand, like everyone else, that this manifesto is one very essential component, which is intended to endure through time and, potentially, accommodate all who dwell within the confines of its letters. And when applied, the contents, it is hoped, will sustain the inherent elements of freedom. But it may not be necessary for you to go searching for answers to your problem in the Constitution because being truly free should not require a search through the Constitution to guarantee the freedom.

Could this possibly be somewhat demanding for the traveler? Perhaps not quite but the Constitution? Perhaps there is no need to search the Constitution for principles that guarantee a person's freedom, but the contents of its letters apparently lend weight and credence to that which upholds both the legal and cultural attributes of freedom.

And here, the traveler seems inclined to admit that the very important presence of the Constitution becomes very critical and paramount as it not only guarantees this freedom but also anchors and upholds both the legal and practical basis of it. It thus lends credence to a people's existence as they live their freedom and defend its utility.

It may dawn on you that one of the very first steps toward finding solutions to some of the social issues facing you in America is to recognize and accept the fact that this is a society made up of various people from various cultures. This realization may encourage the awareness that any changes to any aspect of the social system must be such that they are broad based enough to accommodate the variety of perspectives and preferences that define the various individuals within the society. Your task of finding solutions can seem like a very impossible undertaking. It may seem so until you remember that your mission is not to change the system as a whole but to contribute to the processes of a positive change.

In essence, you embrace the American system and you admire the structure. You appreciate the intent and you laud its resiliency. But you regret the blemish and you seek rectification. For in the end, the inherent benefits of a system should be readily extensible to all its subjects.

And as you wonder if you really found a solution, your mind rehearses the process of your search. Is it deterministic? You wonder! Or is it instinctual and merely predicated on emotion? But you seem quite OK with it, for something tells you it's all predicated on experience, albeit not exactly pleasant. At this point, it is necessary to do some soul searching and validate the utility of your action. You are judging the system and its merits, and you want to make sure that your efforts are not marred by personal biases couched on unwavering stringency. In addition, you may have to check your own mind to guarantee its efficacy and rationality. As it is, besides the difficult issues you are dealing with, there are numerous other factors in America, social and personal, that impact your senses. It is a complex system in a highly charged environment; and, like most of the folks here, yours could be a very loaded mind.

As you proceed to check the quality of your mind and guarantee its soundness, you may toy with the thought of taking off for a while and leaving it all behind, only for a while but long enough to guarantee a refreshed mind. In your newly adopted American society, the people have a word about *going away* and what great good that does to your being.

And as you head out beyond your area, you plan a peaceful moment, almost a perfect escape, so you can lose yourself in the difference of a distant other place. This way, you can really leave it all behind and you can wallow in the tardiness of unhurried moments and the seeming magic, which awakens your senses to the rapture of

> another scene;
> its difference,
> and
> the novelty,
> about
> the quiet style—
> of its people,
> and
> every instance
> that makes it be.

You are on vacation, you remind yourself, as a faint sense of guilt worries your almost decadent mind. And this vacation is truly deserved if only for these few days before you head back to your locale and its maddening process of existence. But you successfully nullify this brief moment of mental subterfusion and unwind to take in the scene. It is your vacation, and it is decidedly stress free and leisurely; the people, the style, the rather rustic roads and their pretense at modernity, and even the natural elements appear to have a preference for tardiness as you take in

> The scene and
> the people;
> the wind—
> in its stressless presence—
> sensuous,
> and
> a tad sassy;
> only sashaying,
> through the scene
> and
> the greenery—
> in
> their rustling sway.

It all touches your senses, and you try not to spoil any aspect of it and aim to take the essence of this beautiful experience as you end your vacation and head back home.

Getting back to your community may require a good effort at a mental switch because the instant change of pace could catch you unprepared and having difficulty making the necessary switch in social perspectives. But since you have no choice but to go with the flow, you let your mind quickly fall into place and begin to deal with the harsh practicalities of your society. You may be slightly thrown off by the seeming rapidity at which some everyday occurrences impact your senses. But you remind yourself that it is only the distinction between what you just left behind and the rush and hustle of what you just returned to. It is in such moments of reentry into the American society that you really appreciate the stress-laden environment you've been living in.

But you are back home. You are back into the grind. And you are back to that place into which you were transplanted either by your own design or some other factor.

This being America, however, just before you can find a moment to catch a breath, events both within and outside your line of occupation propel you into action. And in an instant, you find yourself worrying about one thing or the other. And if you just happen to be unlucky, someone, some character, is poised to throw something unpleasant your way. On some rather rare occasions, however, you may be just lucky enough to have something pleasant come your way. In such cases, your reaction may depend precisely on what good stuff comes your way. If it's money, hold fast and make the most of it. If it is romance, well, a previous experience may determine your response. But if you've had no previous romantic experience in America, as your neighbors would tell you, you take it with caution. These romances often come with strings attached and very, very long strings at that.

In your adopted American society, you've come to rest with the fact that things move at a very fast pace; and at times, events move in such a rapid pace that the sheer rapidity of passage becomes dizzying and leaves you wondering if it is possible to keep up. But back from your vacation means a return to the usual from a brief time out. You immediately find the point at which you left your activities; you find your cues and move on.

You may not exactly return to the very issue you were dealing with before you took off, but you can hardly stay away from it. But because your time out has the potential of providing you with a fresh perspective, you increase your efforts and look for what you can gain from your endeavors.

Well, you admit to yourself that it is not easy to change the American system or any part of it. But you also appreciate the fact that, in this society, it is not exactly the best strategy to let yourself be a victim, particularly as a response to a racially injurious experience. It may not pay to pretend that what you are dealing with—in this case, ethnicity—is no longer there and choose to proceed with a mind of suspended judgment. The very attempt at this will leave you feeling rather unfulfilled as an individual; and by its nature, such pretense will suggest the presence of a person drifting through life and its complexities by choosing to discountenance the unsavory elements that diminish the quality of his life in America. But even if you are good in carrying on with such pretense, the frequency of the occurrence of this social problem could undermine your resolve.

Your best bet could be to begin with self-affirmation and effectively establishing your own identity. It is possible that your steadfast utilization of this stance will generate a confidence that carries you through most of these social problems. And as a transplant in America or even born here, the problem may not be you, your ethnicity, or your presence. It should also be clear to you and your neighbor that your very presence adds to that rich tapestry of ethnic distinctions that otherwise makes it a remarkably outstanding society.

As an individual, however, you are free to look at things your own way. But like it is for some people, a positive opinion of yourself may be difficult to entertain, in which case, the problem just might not be anything with the system. It is not your neighbor either. And if such negative self-perception happens to be one of your primary attributes, well, your adopted society has a name for the kind of professional you need to see.

You might wonder if a negative self-perception really explains your difficulty with some of the social issues you are dealing with in America, particularly if you strongly believe you have no problem with self-perception. You may also wonder if you are alone in feeling this way or perhaps you know a few people in your community who have similar experience. There may be some validity in your thinking because there are social issues in this society that could have strong impact on you despite your self-assurance. Nevertheless, a positive view of yourself helps a great deal. Invariably, your investigations will bring you to the realization, as you probably must have done before, that you do have a role to play as a member of the society. In the process of doing your own part as a member of the society, your positive attitude, therefore, keeps you above the fray. It's like knowing that, in order to sustain a mind-set of social decency, you've chosen to remain head and shoulders above the pettiness of ethnocentric preoccupations.

In the end, you may not be running away from the rather difficult issue of ethnicity but finding an effective way to live and deal with something you've come to suspect could be an intrinsic part of the system.

Or is it?

As you struggle with the social problem of ethnicity in America and as you begin to find your way of dealing with it, however, you may wonder how you live with those times when ethnic discrimination stands in your way to a financial or economic freedom. After all, this too is guaranteed to every person in your adopted society. This may be one of those instances when this societal blemish of racial discrimination

IKE C. UDEH

becomes difficult to live with. On its face, it may seem quite impossible to surmount this problem, and its impact could not only inflame your sense of justice but also paralyze your efforts by weakening your spirits.

And this too you have to overcome.

Still, there is wonder and there are questions. But are they really questions? You, apparently, are placed; or rather, it is a nondefinite instance the apparent essence of which appears to indicate you are not exactly in America. Perhaps you are somewhere, somewhere that seems to place your tangible form in one particular location. And yet there is nothing mysterious about this—for there are no mysteries.

But being you—essentially, being human—there is the tendency to place yourself, your being and, really, the very essence of your humanness, in a place, a place as defined by its boundaries and limits. And since you, as a particular being, started with a particular mind-set of locating your form, your corporal form in a place, a particular place, your impressions and beliefs find you supposedly at this one particular place. Your person then rides along with this mental disposition that sees, or rather, is inclined to place your whereabouts in America.

So you ride along and proceed in this state of nonbeing that has no mysteries and yet no logical explanations for your current situation.

It may behoove you to take a good look around you, and you'll find examples of transplanted folks like you and yet others who have made it despite what might have seemed to be impossible odds in America. Perhaps you'll then realize that this could be one of the easiest of your problems to overcome in America. It could be because as a society whose essence rides firmly on the flow and ebb of the dollar, everyone, including your enemy, wants to do business with you. And as you do business with him, the fact may play in your private thoughts that this is strictly business, and as far as you know, this person doesn't give a crap about you or your well-being. He may pretend to care somewhat but only insofar as whatever be your occupation prospers. That way he stands a good chance of making another dollar off you. This general need to make money, therefore, makes it possible for you to realize financial success. The only obstacle to your success, therefore, could be you.

OK, you've made the money, you are riding quite high in your economic/financial success, but now you feel the need to live in one of those areas where safety, decent schools, and all other resources abound. Then you embark on a search for a better home. In keeping with the general practice, you contact a real estate agent who sounds so delighted you called that he can't wait to see you. He is even more delighted because he's read the signs that suggest you are pretty loaded. In your excitement, you take the trip to meet him. And perhaps you are riding in one of those vehicles that tend to announce your higher economic status, and dressed somewhat appropriately.

Be prepared to be entertained with exceptionally loud and pretentiously accommodating salutation. This is often adorned with a handshake that seems not to want to let go of your hand, including an affected grin designed to mask a sentiment of prejudice. He may ask you several times about your family despite the fact that you already told the bastard you are single; and, of course, he is quick to apologize, only to ask you once again before the meeting is over.

At this point, it is to your best interest not to let the moment get to you because there could be more interesting and oddly entertaining stuff to come.

Going through your papers and personal information may not present any problems because you did your homework and you've got the dough. You then tell him precisely what you want and what location. He is courteous enough to take you around and show you several places ready for sale, but you suspect your escort is emphasizing mostly those places where he's been told to take those of your ethnic background. Now you are wondering if this person has a different agenda or is slightly hard of hearing. As you begin to voice your dissatisfaction, he decides to bring you to one of those places you had indicated you liked. Then you sit and do the paperwork, but he is quick to remind you that nothing can be finalized yet, not even if you are paying cash.

You should not be surprised if your agent calls you first thing the next day to inform you that unfortunately that piece of real estate is sold. "I wasn't aware of that, and my boss just brought it to my attention," he claims. And in an attempt to counter any suspicion of discrimination, he quickly offers you an alternative that, you guessed it, lies within an area he and his folks have decided is proper for your kind.

Now you've got food for thought, and you really wonder if this is the American freedom you heard so much about. You've got the tools, you've got the decency, you've got the money, but you are still very much limited in your freedom and you are still subject to being accorded the opportunity only to play the second fiddle in most social interactions. Can this be frustrating? You have to search me for an answer!

But please don't go burning your dollars yet.

You may need to look around and do some investigation. Chances are there is some real estate agent who hasn't done much business lately. His personal bills are mounting, and a rather angry band of creditors is fast on his track or his estranged partner just cleaned him out. The local folks will often advise you to give this guy a call. Oh yes, you have to make that call because, in his desperation he will sell you anything, even right next to the White House.

And, of course, no need to ask him how he did it, especially since the last agent you dealt with couldn't sell you a shack in the boonies. You take the jewel and count your blessings. If, however, you wake up one morning and find a cross burning across your lawn, you do not need to panic! You call the fire department and give them a description and license plate of the prejudiced real estate agent. Chances are he knows who did it.

Even when you begin to feel quite settled in your newly acquired place of dwelling, you may not feel totally at ease until you learn to convince yourself that not all those persons who frown and curse at the sight of your nice house are necessarily prejudiced. Some are simply envious of you, and their cursing and swearing are simply a clear evidence of misplaced frustration and disappointment. Among such persons could even be some from the same ethnic background as you. After all, you've often heard the people say there is always something about your success your neighbor doesn't like.

But as the traveler wonders about this aspect of human behavior, the instance gets you searching to see if you've really been able to actually place yourself in one particular place. The traveler opts for noninvolvement as he'd prefer to let undefinable instances play themselves out in there nonmysterious ways.

As you work your way through the complications of these social issues in America, it may behoove you to proceed with care because experience may also tell you that every unpleasant interaction with another person does not have to be an instance of prejudice. In this, your newly adopted society, like your society of birth, there will be instances of serious disagreements, angry exchanges that border on the socially uncivil, including periods of apparent threats that may leave you unnerved. Like every other human society, this one also has its share of indecent human interactions. If in the process of transplanting yourself you had an expectation of societal perfection, you may want to get your head off the clouds so you can stay within the confines of realism.

IKE C. UDEH

CHAPTER VIII

The People You Meet

I N HIS SILENCE, the traveler could hear the sound of his own voice! Is it his voice? he wonders! He listens further, a tad more intently; then he seeks to block his hearing simply by sheer will and discountenancing the presence of the sound. He would prefer to let whatever plays within play itself out; and in the end, as it fades into its quiet, its absence will only satisfy the essence of its being:

> Nothing plays,
> And nothing sounds;
> there are no mysteries and—
> There is nothing except—
> The mystery of *nothing*.

And perhaps, you are here, in your new environ, experiencing the newness and, perhaps, somewhat dismayed by your inability to grasp it all as quickly and rapidly as you'd wish.

But the traveler thinks that as you may have realized, your adopted American society obviously has a lot to offer, including the fact that the sky still remains the limit for you and everyone else, provided you are quite prepared to roll up your sleeves and get to work. You decide what appeals to you, which invariably coincides with what you are capable of doing in terms of occupation. You plan your work and aim to work your plan.

In order to stay focused, however, you remain cautious and keep your thoughts on the goal. You will meet and interact with the various persons from different backgrounds who make up the population. You will hear the busy and determined. You will encounter the slightly lazy, who may be independently wealthy. You watch out for these, for they will often give the impression that life is a comfortable walk in a garden of roses. You will also meet some who have chosen to wear the garb of the socially persecuted and forever tortured by what they consider to be the ruling class and the system.

With this group of self-anointed victims, you will often find it impossible to hold a healthy and meaningful conversation. This is not necessarily because they lack the tools for such conversations but because they've chosen to dwell permanently in the past; they will often sound apathetic as they wallow in the constraining delusions of persecution. These will always have someone other than themselves to blame for their misfortunes. They seem always prepared to explain any instance of failure that might come their way as a purposeful design cleverly woven into the system to undermine their attempts at upward mobility. For most of these folks, blaming the system becomes a substituent element for some frustrating personal deficits.

With this kind, you are careful not to let their tortured presence drag you into undeserved pity and the attendant discomfort often elicited by their defeatist utterances. You will get nowhere with them. You get dragged down and thrown off track if you entertain their self-ordained plight. On the other hand, you are viewed as a sellout if you refuse to let yourself be drawn into their view of persistent self-pity and self-righteousness, particularly if you hail from the same ethnic background as they do.

You may decide to stress a few points with these folks, perhaps suggest some way out and emphasize the need to recognize the presence of some unfairness in the American system, but not to let that realization become the obstacle to success. But you want to be aware of the fact that this attempt to encourage a healthier perspective on life may not go down comfortably with your listener. You may also not want to spend your time wondering what went wrong because their behavior is an instance of personal choice and preference. And, yes, this too is another instance of freedom. As the system has it, you can set your goals and get busy or you may choose to dwell permanently on the shortcomings of the society and walk around with a countenance of the eternally oppressed. Oh yes, it's all permissible within the system.

IKE C. UDEH

It is not possible for you to always find those persons who see the blemishes in your adopted society but manage to rise above it all and focus on their goals. And as a transplanted citizen, you need people such as these around you, at least for their encouraging presence. You will need all the strength and support you can muster, and you will need these as frequently as you dare not imagine. The trick is to find some of that support from within yourself. And finding such personal strength is very necessary, particularly since, like everyone else, you learn to fend for yourself. And being a transplant does not suggest an exceptive instance of existence that entitles you to a life of guaranteed social support.

As you deal with whatever shortcomings you experience in the American system, you also remain cognizant of your own perceptions of all that goes on around you. You may be surprised to learn that, as you judge your neighbors and the society as a whole, your interpretations of events are also judicable; and an honest investigatory look at them may leave you a little uneasy. You may find that, despite your perceived personal attributes of social consciousness, transparent magnanimity, and preference for fairness, you also harbor some unhealthy prejudices. These will often play themselves out in those seemingly private moments when an unflattering racial "joke" is made, ostensibly employed to make a point and viewed as totally innocent. And besides, you may be hard-pressed to justify those occasions on which you insisted on letting only your own kind participate and benefit from an incident designed to be enjoyed by everyone, which literally means anyone.

In addition, a further search into your actions and utterances may reveal prejudicial behaviors you exhibit on occasion. It is possible that you'll find reason enough to explain and justify them and thus make yourself feel comfortable with them. So then, as an individual, it should begin to dawn on you that you don't have to be too judgmental as you analyze the society and define the system. You also do not have that exclusive right to judge others as you see fit and expect not to be judged. After all, precisely what gives you the right to condemn others when you make racial jokes and exhibit prejudicial behavior, which are nonetheless a manifestation of clannish and prejudicial inclinations?

Incidentally, if you take a very good look around, you may notice that quite often, it is some of those same persons who scream racism at the dawn of every misfortune that tend to be clannish, discriminatory, and condescending toward others. And as a recent transplant in America, it may not surprise you to learn that a good number of these folks are among the recent arrivals. Some of these people will cite a perceived need for comfort for the reason they rarely associate with others from outside their group, but they rarely have an answer for why they are quick to blame others for the same practice. You get the feeling these people want to have it both ways; it is as if such group comfort is necessary and beneficial only for their kind.

Attempts at selective interaction and socialization may not necessarily be bad, particularly when it occurs as an activity within the continuum of regular everyday human interaction. But it suggests unsavory implications when such activity becomes a conscious act designed to isolate and view others as not so worthy or ethnically below acceptance.

In this, your adopted American society, you will be privileged to experience life as a sophisticated drama played out in all its various forms of complications with far-reaching implications. You may choose to go it slow with minimum interactions with others. You may also choose to get involved in all that appeals to you, and you may decide to rush through the scene, consciously working hard to not let the unpleasant affect your mood. But whichever way you decide to live your life in America, you will still find that you can hardly escape the difficulties, the misfortune and the misstep, which often follow any fortune. Yes, indeed, in this as well as in most human societies, it often seems like every occasion of good fortune is always followed by something unpleasant. And often, such moments of unpleasantness make it rather difficult for the individual to appreciate periods of blessings, such as taking a good look around and being able to notice that, despite whatever plagues him, there is still something to be thankful for.

As a transplant, you may have the benefit of being able to see aspects of the culture that some may not see or simply take for granted. Some of these aspects of the culture are impressive and satisfying to experience and some may be rather difficult to grasp. It is difficult to grasp the essence of the system when you see segregation overtly or covertly played out in grand scale while the ongoing mantra celebrates the culture as the ultimate in a system of social melting pot.

You may find yourself working hard not only to fit in but also to carve out a personal niche that encompasses all the tools necessary for meeting your needs. And while you are at it, it is easy to find yourself veering away from some of the principles you thought you set to guide you and determine the way you interact with others. In this society, you will find that it is necessary to have a set of guiding principles because this helps you as you seek to negotiate through the system and its complexities. But experience invariably will tell you that, as you work through the day and plow through the inherent demands of the system, your method of operation may not always work in concert with the dictates of your principles.

For some, it all gets rather complicated here. It becomes a question of deciding which ultimately holds the key to your being happy: abandoning your principles and going for broke or sticking to your principles and letting the satisfaction therein be something to savor as a preamble to personal happiness. Perhaps for you, happiness may be something you cherish but you are not necessarily willing to go out of your way to experience it. It may be a sentimental instance woven into the personal choices of perception, interpretation, and definition that you assign to circumstances which impact your life. In this case, a not-so-pleasant occurrence may be mentally reconfigured as to minimize its impact. You take it in stride, so to speak, and the eventual transcendence becomes a personal triumph whose moment you savor and cherish. This instance for you becomes a personal experience of satisfaction, a mental gratification evidenced by its corollary of personal happiness. And in this culture, as an individual, you will always need all the feelings of happiness and mental gratification you can create for yourself.

But this is a rather complicated system in a very demanding society. When you do find happiness, your moment of happiness may be short-lived, its brevity dictated by incidents beyond your control. For some, this very brief moment of happiness becomes a transient experience of gratification, which is immediately replaced by the unpleasant, the irritating, and the depressing feeling of disconcertion. For some, it is a moment of mental paralysis guaranteed to retard their efforts at finding happiness. And yet, others would view this as an illuminating occurrence that only crystallizes that aspect of the American culture that tends to negate personal happiness and fosters personal discomfort, mental disequilibrium, and a perennial feeling of uncertainty and apprehension. Some would even go a little further and find themselves flirting with the nascent touches of recurrent paranoia. In its rather severe form, this experience nudges them just slightly out of sync in their mental disposition as they inexplicably find themselves barely holding it together at the threshold of mental dislocation.

You may not exactly find honest pity from the neighbors if you happen to find yourself in this predicament. At the initial onset of your mental impairment, your encounter with a neighbor may present you as the lazy, who purposely courts failure in order to elicit pity and ultimately qualify for a handout.

And, yes, this also is a function of a hostile dog-eat-dog environment, which makes each person suspicious of the other. You are expected to always pick yourself up by the bootstrap and march along, your personal predicament notwithstanding. But, of course, when the mind is slightly dislocated, picking oneself up by the bootstrap becomes a laborious attempt at a seemingly simple task that is immediately transformed into an impossibly onerous undertaking by the errant perceptions of a fractured mind.

Often, as you marvel at the seeming magic that typifies some of the modern wonders around you, you find yourself also wondering just why so much could possibly be so wrong with the whole system. Taken in isolation and allowed to play effectively in your head, this perception could be very discouraging at the very least. But viewed in perspective, the incidence of the American system as a human design may allow for some of the disturbing failures in the system. But does it really?

The traveler demurs.

One thing is sure: along with working hard toward your goal, the nature of the American system also requires you to work hard at maintaining your sanity. This is one task you have to really do alone.

If you are lucky to hold your mind together and stay in step with both the personal and social demands, your task of working toward your goal becomes an undertaking invariably defined by what you set as goals. And as you busy yourself with what you've defined as important, your whole being is also being redefined as a person. Chances are, as an individual, you are not exactly that same person who left one society for another in search of a better life. As this happens, you often find it difficult to tolerate some of the things you used to be able to live with. And incidentally, you may not quite realize the change in you until you are faced with a situation that brings an incident from the old culture right into the current one. Such experience may not even tell you in detail how much you have changed because you are still you but essentially a different you.

Even as you quarrel with some aspects of the American culture, you could still find yourself often defending everything about it, particularly when you find yourself being criticized as being too Americanized. This often happens when you have a new arrival from the old culture who may have to depend on you for quite a while for his livelihood.

For some transplants in America, this could be a very difficult situation to deal with. The new arrival settles in with totally different views, albeit those same views you shared when you were back in the old culture. If this new fellow happens to be bunking at your place, you can expect friction and disagreements, which steadily worsen as the stay continues. The new arrival may find it difficult to understand why you have very limited time to sit and chat. He can't grasp your definition of time including your rather foreign interpretation of everything, particularly the personal. It becomes either annoying to him or simply an unnecessary instance of show off when he notices your apparent short attention span. The rift widens when you begin to complain about the cost of harboring him, including how much of your time you feel is necessary to make him feel welcome.

First it is your "rush, rush, I have to go" attitude that sets the unsavory tone; and subsequently, the "I am too busy to chat" body language begins to create undesired separation between you and your guest. In time, your person, as perceived by your guest, including the disposition that defines your presence, becomes a source of disconnect, which leaves your guest feeling unwelcome.

The traveler would rather be left out of this! This is perhaps best left to you, your guest, and your conscience.

At this point, you can try to explain all you want and it simply won't do. And the more you find yourself trying to explain your actions and the conditions, which make them unavoidably necessary, the more irritated you find yourself.

As for the guest, the most disturbing aspect of your behavior could be your definition of interpersonal relationship, particularly if this guest is a close relative. But you've assimilated; and for you, like the neighbors, self-sufficiency and the ability to fend for yourself has become a learned experience, which is seen as being very necessary for your survival. Not so with your guest, whose perspectives are still akin to the old culture; and the vitality of his expectations are culled from the customs of the old culture. It is not uncommon for the guest to write home and complain to any willing listener and narrate how monstrous your attitude has become. And that's one way most of the folks back in some other cultures get the impression that this society corrupts rather than improve the individual's behavior, the fact that they are basing their judgments on the complaints of a disgruntled guest notwithstanding.

Somewhere in the midst of all this, however, there is a nagging feeling of guilt that dogs you every time you return home from your occupation; and this feeling also generates frustration. Something in you appears to understand where your guest is coming from, but the constraints of a difficult system in a society that constantly advocates the principles of survival of the fittest undermine any inclination to truly appreciate his views. It is impossible to elevate his views to the level of comfortable acceptance because your life is driven by the strident demands of the culture and its system. Space, including relationships, other than the romantic, becomes things you've begun to define in relation to your needs. Perhaps in your romantic relationship, space, need, and time are being defined from a coexistential standpoint, which allows for a mutuality of perspectives. But throw into your daily life a live-in person with different sets of values and expectations, and you find yourself at odds with some of those perspectives you once shared and cherished.

And, of course not, you are not quite a monster—at least not yet—until things get so ugly and unbearable that you begin to send the message to your guest that you want him to find a place of his own. Now, seen through the lenses of the old culture, you've really done it. You've crossed the line, and as far as your guest and his sympathizers are concerned, you are a monster or something quite close to it. And, by the way, in some families, this act is simply unpardonable. For you to have the nerve to become so Americanized that you have the audacity to put this guest out of your place means you must have forgotten your roots so badly that you've become a source of shame to the family. In some cases, it might even be deemed necessary for the family back home to consider some form of sacrifice because the perceived oracular benefits could help to rescue you from the stranglehold the "nonhuman" ways of the Yankee have on you.

Incidentally, situations such as these have been indicated to take a rather drastic turn for the worse. And since the sacrificial exercise back home is being sustained, your mind, steeped in the belief of the power of the oracle, invariably struggles with the constraints of its reach and shudders at the prospects of its own impotence. As this rather unsavory experience degenerates, the vanishing shadows begin to take on a more menacing form, their gait seeming like a tangible threat, made more ominous by the perceived potency of their apparent presence.

Since your origin is based in the old culture and its practices, you may begin to wonder precisely what happens next, particularly if you in any way subscribe to the belief that such oracular undertakings could affect your life. And God help you if you think you are beginning to see things. Oh yes, some strange characters, humanlike in gait and form, have been pacing the hallways and vanishing into the walls as you try to catch a nap. And by the time you begin to believe that nonexistent shadows are following you, you know it is time to look for a more viable alternative to your current lifestyle—Yankee ways or no damn Yankee ways! You guessed it, such change is particularly necessary at this juncture because you'd be hard-pressed to find any redemptive help, not even from the local magician otherwise known as shrink! And like a lot of the assimilated transplants in America, if on top of all this you haven't at any moment made peace with some force or forces, maybe a creator beyond and above you and your fellow humans, then your situation is not simply beyond help but also deplorably beyond redemption.

If you so much as entertain any doubts as to the propriety of your actions when you put out your guest and begin to doubt the sanity of your mind, some of your actions may seem so odd to you that you begin to wonder if others are beginning to see you as having lost your mind; worse still, you begin to suspect that some among your detractors are rejoicing over your apparent demise. But you do not need to worry since if your mind is actually beginning to fail, you may not be able to tell exactly who the hell is jumping for joy and who doesn't give a damn. It is all part of the mix in the American system; whatever you do, there is always something or someone ready to make you doubt the propriety of your action.

Amid all this, the indefinite nature of your position, the location of your corporal form remains what it is—and the traveler? Perhaps it is a situation that could only find any logical explanation from you, and so the traveler seems rather inclined to let it be that way. And your guest?

And now the traveler shifts, seemingly, as his apparent form moves just slightly, perhaps only minimally as he wonders aloud soundlessly:

> If your being remains a void,
> And the position of your person shows no specific locality;
> Your corporal *self* not placed or situated in a particular place;
> And you have a guest;
> Does your guest become part of and dwell in your void?

Perhaps you are lucky enough to find that your mind did not exactly lose its footing. It only touched the outer borders of insanity and briefly peeked through its scary confines. But essentially, your mind remains quite Okay. So the next item for consideration is convincing yourself that you made a sound and reasonable decision as demanded by an economic exigency by putting out your guest. The American system is such that it requires that you know the limits of your financial capability and make sure that you stay within the bounds of these limits. As a caring person, you are always ready to offer help, particularly to a new arrival, who may be in need. But as you already know, this is a society in which knowing one's financial capabilities requires the individual to work in accordance with his own personal capacities. The alternative to this practice often finds the individual sliding into financial difficulties. And in the end, you find yourself marching backward on the economic track.

The beauty of your firm decision is that it doesn't take much time for your guest to begin to understand the situation you were in, because no sooner does he begin to earn a living than he begins to experience the demands and the pressures that come from a plethora of responsibilities. He quickly learns how time, space, work, and play are all interwoven so intricately that life in America becomes a remarkably uneasy undertaking. And, of course, when he throws his earnings into the picture, he finds that this undertaking involves a rather treacherous journey that places enormous demands on his senses. He soon finds that having to respond appropriately to these demands leaves no room for additional responsibilities. With this realization, it begins to dawn on him that this is a very different culture, a very different system from what he was used to in the old culture and one that tends to dictate the process of participation for the individual. As he learns how to work with the American system, he begins to carve out his own niche. He finds his cue and marches along, and it's all within the process of assimilation.

Now you've got another transplant, albeit one from the same old culture as you; and like you, he is beginning to assimilate. The interesting thing about assimilation in America is that the more you assimilate, the more a part of you yearns for the old system and wants to hold fast on to that which you now feel has more significance than you realized. And in moments when you feel somewhat under the weather from the various responsibilities facing you, such yearnings become exacerbated by nostalgia. As the resident folks always say, every American has two heritages. But for the transplant, awareness of this dual attribute becomes a disquieting prehension that is crystallized by the inadequacy of his feelings. He feels the need to hold on to the old culture and, thereby, attributes inordinate significance to its system and begins to endow it with rather superfluous qualities. He believes he is very much in touch with the old system, but he is not exactly packing up and heading back and often finds himself struggling with mutually exclusive mental dispositions.

In the midst of his quandary, the transplant begins to find fault with his adopted culture, and every unfortunate incident that falls in his path is exaggerated and becomes another factor that diminishes the quality of the American culture.

But since he is not exactly packing up and heading out, his feelings about any diminishment in the quality of his adopted society become essentially transient. He may even discard the feelings by consciously holding fast to those factors in the American culture, which not only made him relocate but also make him want to broaden his niche. In the end, he would have substituted affirmation for negation. And this he finds quite possible because his perceptions of being in touch with the old system were purely abstract sentiments, often sufficient as occasional predilections to satiate the occasional feeling of nostalgia.

CHAPTER IX

The Transformation

H ERE, THE TRAVELER suspects that you've probably wondered about how really varied some of those people you meet are as you busy yourself with whatever be your occupation. But as you meet other people, other people as well meet you and as they size you up, some may not be very familiar with what they see in your person. Actually, this is just as true in the American system as in other cultures.

What people see in you may not necessarily be that same person who emigrated from one society and relocated here. You may see exactly the same person you've always seen even before you left your old society; but the truer picture of you is that person with a much changed perspective on things, particularly social issues, and a person who's been transformed by experiences that are very different from what you knew and felt in your old society. What others see when they meet you, however, is mostly determined by some preformed opinion about your kind, including how you impress them. The stronger determining factor for others as they meet you in America, however, is your ethnic background. Depending on the color of your skin, at first meeting, your presence may evoke an odd mixture of apprehension, some awe, a touch of misplaced surprise, and a guarded welcome couched on evident unctuosity. Or it may be a first meeting that evokes some of the above adorned with affected smiles and a tinge of pity that seems to flow from a guarded presence.

In your initial experiences, when you first arrive in America, you may not immediately detect these feelings from some of those people you meet. And this could be because your previous culture had taught you to be warm, welcoming, and sincerely appreciative of others, particularly those that appear to be so very friendly at first meeting. But in time, you learn that this seemingly friendly posture from others is something you take with a lot of caution. You learn how not to be so gullible. You learn the tricks inherent in baring your teeth in pretentious smiles while whispering to yourself, *What a terrible person* or *What an asshole* or a combination of both.

As you learn and get to know the American culture and how the society operates, your experiences begin to force a change in you. And as your experiences broaden, you gradually shed most of those factors that shaped your person and your perspectives in your old culture. Your views on social issues, relationships, interactions with others, and how you perceive others gradually change in accord with your current experiences.

> Transformation in progress?
> Oh yes;
> And this,
> Is the process!

On some occasions, you may meet some of those people who genuinely appreciate meeting someone from a different culture. You can often tell these folks from the ease, the obvious absence of insecurity, the brief but sufficient smile, and the comfort about their person as they exchange greetings with you. These persons would often show genuine interest in chatting with you, not necessarily as something exotic but as a person with a different cultural background and ultimately unique in his own way.

As a transplant in America, you may find that such honestly friendly people often have had more direct contacts with others from a different culture, or it may be that some of these people are naturally comfortable with themselves and very secure in their persons. Consequently, such persons aren't dressed in pretentious garbs stitched with threads of insecurity and unctuous sincerity. They are nicely self-assured, comfortable in themselves, and quite comfortable around others.

You begin to see some of those things that are responsible for your transformation when you consider the fact that, in order to blend in and to survive in America, it is necessary for you to adopt some of those social mores, which define the mode of social interactions. You do not want to leave yourself vulnerable in most situations, particularly those in which any sign of gullibility from you leaves you open to condescending remarks. Such remarks may take the form of making you feel as though you are less civilized while seeming to give your opponent the air of superiority. And you can often tell such occasions from the rather vulgar laughter and comments, which seek to demean your person while pretending to show an interest in you, your old culture, and your ethnicity. And you can sense the start of such occasions because the vulgarity and uncouthness are often very apparent.

The detractors of the American culture often say that these rather unfriendly and impolite behaviors are among the various factors indicative of a society devoid of genuine humanity and driven by excess greed at the expense of true human communion. They point to what they see as lack of warmth, avarice, and cutthroat individualism as the basis of relationships and condemn the apparent need for one individual to take advantage of the other, so long as the end result benefits the one at the detriment of the other. In such instances, it is claimed, the victim is left to deal with his misfortune as his opportunistic neighbor gloats about his ingenuity while treating his victim's pains as a sign of weakness. The more the pain, the more the opportunist cherishes his apparent success. With a hardened heart, he is able to live with such callous treatment of his neighbor and seemingly thrives on his discomfiture. Ultimately, he minimizes his neighbor's pains as he further relates to him with an air of condescension.

But you wonder if these detractors of the American system are not stretching their point rather too far as you examine the makeup of every human society there is and consider the fact that each and every one of these societies has its own blemishes; each has its own imperfections and most certainly a good number of such opportunists among its population.

But as you assimilate, it may not be the easiest task for you to try to always eschew those behaviors that could make you appear cold and unfeeling toward your neighbor. You may need to stay constantly conscious of your actions and your motives as you relate to others.

At some point, you may even begin to wonder why it seems to take literally no effort on your part to become so transformed. Then you get to the point where you also wonder about those factors mostly responsible for your transformation. You realize and appreciate the need to blend. You feel the process of blending involves doing as the citizens do, and you adopt a good portion of the culture because you feel it is the only way to play your part in social situations—because this meets the general expectations. You then get to a point where you begin to wonder where to draw the line and wonder what gives and what's worth your while because it makes sense to you and fits the picture of what you expect from others. Despite the appearance of finding yourself in a quandary, you find answers to your questions because experience has a way of providing answers in such moments when answers are badly needed.

What you settle for may not necessarily be in accord with what you'd rather prefer; but in the end, you realize that, in America, it isn't what suits your sentiments that matters but that which suits the moment and meets your social needs in a particular situation.

Part of being a well-rounded transplant is not simply knowing when and why to lay blame and on whom to place the blame but also knowing when it becomes necessary and proper to place blames. As a transplant, you'll find it often seems rather too easy to blame and castigate some persons or a particular group for most and, often, all the ills that dog the society and diminish its qualities. This is often true at times when every social ill is blamed on the Caucasian group. This becomes disgustingly troubling when it is very apparent that the ill in question had nothing to do with the group or vice versa. And you find that such rather convenient blames, often tend to undermine the prospects of cordial and respectful interracial interactions. This is particularly true in private, person-to-person interactions when both parties are familiar with each other or simply meeting as mere acquaintances; in its rather more honest instance, the parties interact on a purely human level, devoid of racial distinctions, and their communications with each other are often couched on the warmth of shared humanity and buoyed by the simplicity of their rather instinctive graciousness.

You begin to appreciate the manner in which you've changed and how significant and necessary the change, when you realize that you are better tuned to the language and nuances people use in most social interactions. It becomes much easier for you to be ready and willing to respond in kind to an incident or action that is disrespectful or demeaning to you. Of course, you are polite, and politeness still remains part of the repertoire, which is available to you in any social interaction.

But this social nicety is only demonstrated when the occasion suggests its appropriateness, and this is particularly the case in your new culture.

In this society, social rudeness and demeaning and disrespectful behavior including indecent racial remarks are not exactly limited only to the unfortunate experiences of black or other nonwhite transplants. But these groups of persons experience such offensive acts more often than other transplants. For the black and brown transplants, the situation is often more offensive and demeaning at least from its more frequent occurrence. As a nonwhite transplant in America, at the initial stages of your relocation, you may be very rudely surprised when such disrespectful acts are aimed at you in situations when you least expect it. These are some of those occasions when in a supposedly peaceful and congenial setting, some wise fellow inches close to you and makes a racially offensive remark.

The racial and other ethnic insults you experience come in various ways through a multitude of sources. At times it comes in the form of a social program, ostensibly instituted for the benefit of the minority. The stated intent of the program may appear to have a socially desirable value; but the method of its utilization, however, may have a not-so-obvious factor, which becomes an institutional tool for identification and categorization.

Identification and categorization? Could there be more to this? Perhaps there are no deliberate acts here, only an error of human failing resulting in a misplacement of a good idea.

The traveler shifts in his apparent discomfort. Or is it discomfort? There was a movement around and about what seems to be his position, his presence not exactly in disconsonance with his form as his being reacts to the currency of the discourse and the potency of its ramifications.

He wavers just a bit in his mind but steadies his thoughts as he notes the apparent dichotomy in human nature; there is the good, there is the fair, there is the bad, there is the downright ugly. Perhaps it's best to focus on the good. But could that leave you very vulnerable?

In time, you find your transformation coming full circle. Not only have you met others—various others, with a variety of quirks, admirable qualities and some distasteful social mores—but you also met yourself.

Oh yes, as a transplant in America, at the farthest confines of your assimilation and transformation, you meet you. You meet a you, which you least expected would emerge when you first settled here. The

IKE C. UDEH

initial encounter between the residual you that is still connected by a weakening string to the old culture and the current you may seem rather strange. But the strangeness is only brief and very transient because this current you is not only a function of transformation but also the inevitable result of total assimilation.

You are now very much a product of the American society, and the person you are now encountering in yourself is a remade person, demanded by the need for conformity and molded by experience. It is a you that has emerged to live in accord with the demands of your adopted society. And your very changed perspective on life and the human species is indeed proper to the American environment in which you are now resident.

This is it. This is the resulting change in personality that follows a change in perspectives.

And as your mind is inclined to believe, this is America. These are those shores that beckoned some time ago with boundless promise and extraordinary potential. The promise was enormous and exceedingly within reach. It was an uplifting element in your thought process, and its meaning seemed remarkably life sustaining. The potential therein was exquisitely attractive and its mention, superlatively seductive. You probably had this somewhat distant fear before you moved that this potential, like all others, had no tangible reality in its purely abstract nature. But the allure, the novelty, and the appealing romance implied by its suggestion overrode your sense of doubt. And probably, you are no worse for being taken by it all.

But you are far, far into your assimilation; and your transformation, along with the good tidings it brought, comes with a tidy package of tangent variables, which ride along as elements of disillusionment. How this impacts you will depend on how this current you defines what is necessary for your existence.

You are, at this point, probably not disillusioned. But there is this realization—that this is America, with its very human environment, and it's all ephemeral, it's all transient as it all passes in fleeting moments of nonenduring American experience. And you suspect that the best way to deal with this thought is to discountenance its presence and live in the moment with a mind that sizes up every instance and seizes the most beneficial course. And, of course, you should be quite inclined to not view such instances of ephemerality as only unique to the American way; it is a human thing, perhaps factored into the nature and the essential makeup of that species termed human in its tangible presence and humanity in its seeming abstraction.

As you assimilate and become more Americanized, you experience some of those factors that define the society often by creating protocols and mores for social interactions. These may not be factors officially sanctioned as codes of interactions, but they play significant roles in a lot of social situations. One of these factors is the manner in which the system defines the various ethnic groups. Some groups are defined from the precepts of basic human criteria that present the groups as very human and very worthy of all the privileges accorded all humans. Along with this definition comes the blessing of priority treatment and attention in all facets of social and personal needs. As a transplant in America, you may not be surprised to see these privileged groups wallowing in the socially created atmosphere of true freedom, greater opportunities, and a tad more protection under the law.

It is not uncommon to find folks from these groups interacting with others with a rather distasteful air of superiority, and some would top it off with a presumed attribute of greater intelligence. Among such characters are some who would steadily qualify for some of the highest awards for dumbness, some could be just slightly above the threshold of patent stupidity, but they all feel quite comfortable and secure in the socially defined criteria that accord them the right and the privilege that entitle them to some very uncouth behaviors with no accountability.

As an individual, it may not be best to blame such people for their ill-informed knowledge of themselves, and you may not even nurture the sentiments that could let their behavior bother you. You become more inclined to pity their persons as you note the unfortunate effect of a regrettable social phenomenon on them. At times, you even have difficulty stopping yourself from attempting to find excuses for the behavior of these folks. And this is often because you find that, for these people, such behavior of assumed superiority has become a means of survival. For some, it is an easy way to mask what they suspect is not their most admirable quality; hence, it behooves them to do their utmost to wear a false presence of superiority.

The traveler considers and analyzes the various behaviors manifested by people. It is as if the more varied the group of people, the more interesting the variety of behaviors one encounters.

IKE C. UDEH

With every group you meet in America, you find a code, often unspoken, with which the society defines the group. You see the adverse effects of some of these codes as you witness how it all fragments the social fabric by creating a hostile element that runs just below the surface of the social platform.

Being a transplant, you are somewhat dismayed by the fact that, in some instances, the system itself appears to sanction the use of such codes either through its pretense at their nonexistence or from its preference for minimizing the social effects of these codes.

You begin to wonder if there is any recourse to this social blemish, particularly if you belong to a group socially classified as minority. But before you begin to busy yourself with the search for explanations and remedies, you find that there is a debate on the social platform regarding race. Then you learn that the debate often follows after a racially charged incident that may be so deplorable it awakens the sense of justice in most decent people, and this, in turn, elicits a feeling of outrage. The discussion heats up, and the media is saturated with talk sessions, often led by various experts who are called up from all corners of the country to give their opinion.

In time, in keeping with the process, the debate degenerates into hyperboles, circumlocutions, and outright non sequiturs. Ultimately, the otherwise horrible incident is effectively dressed down to unpleasant generalities within the social structure in need of some minor fixes. You watch the debate fade into silence as the experts disappear into their comfortable quarters. The incident lapses into the quiet of the past. The victim is left to lick his wounds. But in actuality, there is more than one victim since whatever was done to him was essentially aimed not simply at him but at his kind, in this case, his ethnic group.

The traveler does not exactly demur as he considers the various angles within the complex nature of interactions among various persons. He knows there is the good, and there is the bad side to every human's behavior; perhaps it is the motivational factor behind the bad behavior that is worth exploring.

As for now, the traveler feels that as you try to fathom the aspect of the system that appears to leave room for the manifestation of such racially motivated acts of hostility, it may be to your amazement when, right at the end of the debate, some honest soul in the process of trying to find real solutions unearths similar or worse incidents. At this point, it may even shock you to learn that these other incidents are occurring as the previous one is being forgotten. Then it begins to dawn on you that the incidents you hear about are only those that make the headlines, either because the perpetrators were exposed or they happen to have occurred right in front of a camera.

Perhaps such racial incident was not directed at your kind but aimed at another one of the groups in the social make up. You even hear statements from some among the unaffected group that appear to blame the victim or victims for being rather closed and clannish. In this case, the victim was targeted because he happened to be from a group that's viewed as being clannish. Now you, as a transplant, are motivated to take a closer look into the makings of racially motivated hostile acts in your adopted society.

Is the driving force behind these acts akin to insecurity and selfishness on the part of the perpetrators? Or is it an evidence of the inability to be socially accommodating of others? You mull over such questions as you search for answers. But you wonder, aren't all groups in the face of sustained persecution inherently clannish at least to the extent that being cohesive and collaborative among themselves affords them the only effectively protective approach to what they see as a clear threat to their very existence? You find yourself more at a loss for answers as you consider the fact that the perpetrators often think alike. They often hail from the same group and tend to lend support to the distasteful actions of others from their group. After all, the perpetrators often carry out their deeds aware of the silent backing of others and emboldened by the prospects of anonymity as sanctioned by others within their group.

But as it is, there is beauty in humanity; and, despite the apparent ugliness in some of its actions, the sheer magnitude of some of its altruistic touch on each other lends credence to the depth of its natural goodness.

As for the traveler, you may be inclined to search his conscience or mind, whichever seems present within the scene. His presence is not clearly defined; his conscience, perhaps void; and the mind, perhaps tailored in concert with an instance of nonpresence. There is no mystery here; there is no tangible substance that defines a form, a being, or other. And the traveler? A mystery? Perhaps it all fits and perhaps not.

But
There is nothing mysterious about everything
But everything mysterious about *nothing*

So it amazes you beyond your imagination that the same group that condemns another for what it perceives as clannishness is, by its own actions, very clannish—in this case, inimically clannish.

Then, as your mind mulls these social dichotomies in America, it wades through the intricacies and sifts through the variables. You search for that which is practical and possible within the confines of its broader application. You shy away from the inadequate precepts of prejudicial judgment and seek answers from thoughtful considerations and the offerings of their abundant possibilities.

Now, you begin to sense the diminishment of frustration in your search. You feel the satisfaction of honest approach to a social problem and sense the tinge of gratification that accompanies a personal debate that seeks to accommodate others, even in the unholy presentation of themselves. You are not being judgmental of those whose actions you disapprove of but seek to explore and figure out what propels some folks toward some of these rather disturbing antisocial behaviors.

But then, somewhere along the line, a rather simple deed played out on the social platform catches your attention. You stop to get the drift, and then you realize it's an interracial action. You don't exactly sing praises, but you are amazed, essentially impressed, because you just witnessed the offering of a timely help from one stranger to another; and on closer inspection, it is one from one ethic group lending a hand to one from another. And this too you count as an experience. This too you add to the plethora of exemplary moments, for it too lends a word to the very essence of America.

Were there rival groups in your old society? Were there warring sects bent on undermining others for their own gain? Perhaps you had what could pass for groups in your old society, but the lines of demarcation were not so strictly drawn and deliberately structured as to impeach any social contract guaranteed by the state. There were no promises either—promises and claims that spoke of perfection and the ultimate in human enterprise. So the situation in your old society may be different in that it essentially presents itself as a human society with all the attendant failings.

Your old society may also define social interactions from a standpoint of much less person-to-person competition. It may not be totally free of blemishes, but the absence of die-hard individualism, which necessitates the mentality of me first at any cost, lends it a somewhat more human touch that tends to mitigate the consequences of interpersonal hostility. And because your old society may not enjoy the level of wealth as does your adopted American, the bitter rivalry and cutthroat competition present in the American society may be absent.

The traveler knows, however, that there is competition among people in every human society, but he wonders if such competitive mind-sets are not more pronounced in this society than in most others. It appears, he surmises, the more advanced and, with more resources at its disposal, the more competitive a society becomes. But he is inclined to view this as a double-sided factor in humanity's approach to managing its existence, the other being the possibility that the more competitive a society is, the more the chances for advancement. Now, whether this apparent bonus is derived by design or inadvertently, the traveler is not about to engage in any debates. This mental disposition remains just fine with him because he is inclined to view humanity as a complex group with far-ranging wants, needs, and motivations often nudged by necessity and shaped by fluid predilections.

But the traveler could admit that, from a purely human standpoint, a good deed from one person to another elicits a very positive response, which often encourages a general feeling of the need to do more. Good deeds often become contagious, particularly when they are done with no strings attached. And this makes you realize that practically every person has the capacity to do good deeds for other persons. You then begin to wonder just why do some people seem to have a preference for doing evil things to others. As an individual, as you witness such indecent people in action, you are inclined to recoil from the sheer ugliness of such actions. But these actions take on added significance when they are done by a person from one racial group to another from a different group. And if you witness such acts more often than you expected, the experience begins to undermine your sense of safety and negate the expectation of amicable coexistence.

The experience then begins to shape your perceptions of the American culture and the system as a whole. Now you are not simply riding along on the promise of cohesiveness and mutual respect among

IKE C. UDEH

the various persons in the society; you are no longer taking for granted that every person you meet has the best intentions for you; and like most of the residents you met in America, you become increasingly cautious and, ultimately, suspicious of your neighbors. You find yourself more often on guard and less altruistic than you might be inclined to be. And there is the added element of preparedness, which creates a disposition of unfriendliness right beneath the veneer of cordiality and social decency. Like other residents around you, you have now become, by necessity, a product of the culture and its system. For a transplant, this new you may be quite at odds with how you were raised and who you really are. But this new you appears to be precisely what the system demands for your survival, and it seems to work just fine.

And incidentally, this strikes right at the basics of the traveler's disinclination to judge others, person or nonperson, a mental preference for neutral disposition in matters of character, behavior, and personal cultures displayed on a social platform.

As a transplant in America, you may not know exactly how this transformation happened. You may not even realize how much you've changed perhaps until you find yourself in a situation in which all you need to be is simply a person. And this could be that moment when you have to interact with another person from the old culture. It could even be a person from this culture who happens to have found a way of not letting the system shape him. During such encounters, as you present your guarded and less trusting self, you find this other person very comfortable with himself and observably relaxed.

This becomes one of those moments when this other person in your presence makes you feel somewhat uncomfortable. You feel this way not because of some untoward behavior from the person but simply because of his assured and relaxed presence that still has a way of letting you know that, along with the comfortable presence, there is the quiet self-confidence that effectively keeps any uncivil character at a comfortable distance. It is a presence that both welcomes and discourages the uncouth from trying anything funny. Your discomfort then may come from a sense of latent confusion from not knowing immediately how to respond in kind and thus be relaxed, less guarded, and more simply a person.

But as it is, you may not exactly be in America; but the nature of you, like most humans, inclines you or your mind to place your physical form at a specific point at any given moment. Perhaps your specific whereabouts is unknown, and wherever you are seems like a situation that remains your own issue to be resolved. And so, it seems something perhaps inexplicable about your person, inclines your mind toward placing your physical form in America.

But the traveler would rather not take this on; he'd let the onus lie where it may and only explore the point that:

There are no mysteries

So for a transplant in America, it is at this point beginning to seem like your journey to these shores has brought on enormous consequences which you hardly imagined. It may not be the sheer enormity of these consequences that jars your experience, but the inherent complexities may leave you rather befuddled and silently searching for your very self. And like everything else in this society, the neighbors may tell you how to find that self. And, oh yes, you guessed it, you'll be referred to that professional, affectionately known as the shrink. As a transplant, at this juncture, you may need some extra preparations for this encounter. Assuming you've decided to see this professional person, be prepared, for it may not be exactly a romantic encounter ordained with easy answers couched on the prospects of immediate relief.

A shrink? Chances are, in your old society, the very mention of a psychotherapist gets the whole damn neighborhood running for cover. But no one needs to blame the folks over there for such reaction because the culture, just like this one, has its own way of defining each and every human experience. But if a person's situation becomes such that a shrink is being suggested, as the word spreads in the neighborhood, everyone now has a viable explanation for any act, any quarrel or disagreement, and every known mistake made by him or any member of his family. This neighborly explanation of the family's transgressions rides on the simple fact that, since this person is crazy, everyone in the family must be crazy. Chances are, back in your old culture there is hardly any formal diagnosis for such human predicaments, so a simple neighborhood explanation tends to settle the matter.

And here, the traveler finds the ease with which to let his mind stretch just slightly beyond the current confine to search through a collection of possibilities; in this attempt, he may perchance reach the instance that may aid him as he utilizes it to compare and contrast the various human cultures. He remains very aware that every human culture has its own shrinks, albeit shrinks as defined and utilized according to the local cultural tenets. There is the Westernized, molded, guided, and dressed in the proper tradition; and there are others—very qualified, fitting and proper for the job, but tending to shy away from the purely Western approach in style and delivery; and then others, by no means the least, whose methods include a touch of the Western, packaged in the local tradition and delivered with a cautionary word of warning from the local deity. And, no, the traveler does not view this as an aberration in this latter form since it is perceived to work; and whatever it delivers is accepted among the local populace as it comfortably fits the paradigm, all kicking of the ball is toward the goal.

So as a transplant in America, when the neighbors echo the warning that the individual must take care of himself and shouldn't get sick, the words ring more true for you. Since in the old society psychotherapy is probably not a very attractive enterprise and could have very terrible implications, keeping your sanity intact in this society becomes an undertaking with the utmost importance, both for your survival and well-being here and for yourself and others elsewhere. The last thing you need is for bad news such as you being insane to reach the folks back home.

Incidentally, such cautionary words of self-protection and care may take on added urgency for you as a transplant because the incidence of a troubled mind immediately implies something horribly contagious, and you just can't quarrel with that, for that's simply how some of the people back there see it.

And then, the traveler breaks for a brief mental recapitulation, a fleeting instance of momentary communion between his form and his being.

It appears the traveler is here; only the traveler perhaps and his shadows. Is there no one else present? He records and analyzes this moment and also every occurrence and the potential of its possible imminence.

It is empty and vacant within, but there is a whisper; it is a barely audible whisper, not exactly from the traveler but from around. Did it sound like a human whisper, a drifting whisper from a differently animate object, or a lonely whisper built into a sibilant sound by the sheer agony of its loneliness? Nothing fades, not the sound perhaps of the whisper. But—

> The traveler is;
> His mind is;
> His thoughts—
> Emptiness;
> Nothing sounds;
> And
> There's a word!
> A hiss,
> And quiet!

Then, silent sound—apparently occasioned not exactly by incident but for the incidence of the sheer weight of emptiness in concert with its own void.

And the traveler wonders, is there sound from nothingness? But there is no one else here; the sound of nothing from nothing could be silently audible. Perhaps there was nothing present. And the whisper?

And apparently, he knows; or rather, the traveler's being grasps the very loaded implications of this moment. It is not a mystery, but both the instance and the significance of its occurrence lack the comfort of logical explanation:

The probability of sound of, and from nothing being audible and it playing not by incident but for the incidence!

CHAPTER X

In God We Trust

THE MORE ASSIMILATED you become, the more you grasp the significance of those things in the culture that once seemed strange to you as a transplant in America. This experience is further enhanced by the fact that the American culture has the exceptionally unique element that at the same time it embraces most of the aspects you find in other human societies, it also has qualities that make it very different from other cultures. As you come to accept these aspects of the culture, the process of Americanization becomes a given. It begins to get rather difficult to distinguish what in your social interactions is directly borrowed from your previous culture from that which is originating from the purely American custom.

One thing that comes into play is the way things are defined in especially person to person interactions. Another is the definition, or interpretation, given to some of those practices which your previous culture held very high in the course of most social interactions. Some cultures outside America might consider it disrespectful for a person to address his older sibling by name, even if the difference in age is relatively small. Yet some other cultures might consider it bad manners for the individual to look directly into the eyes of an older person or address his or her parent while looking directly at the parent. This practice is a custom that demands that the young fellow places his hands folded behind his back, facedown, in the presence of the older person or his parents. This custom may even require the younger person to either get down on her knees, as a female, or lie facedown, as a male, before the parent or adult, especially in salutations.

Seen from the Western perspective, such humble presentation of oneself is rather subservient; and, at times, when the younger person avoids eye contact, the poor fellow could be deemed to be hiding or attempting to hide something from the adult. In simple terms, this younger person who would not make eye contact could be lying and, therefore, guilty of some transgression.

So what stands as a humble and respectful process, the absence of which could be viewed in one culture as a disrespectful instance of impertinence, is interpreted in the another system as either being subserviently bashful or an attempt to hide a pair of lying eyes.

As an Americanized transplant, for some, it becomes rather difficult to translate this remarkable custom of salutation into a process worthy of maintaining in the American society. But it totally isn't that easy either. Maintaining this practice in the American system becomes alien at best and ridiculously out of place at worst. And besides, the American culture emphasizes eye-to-eye contact whether in a salutatory process of communication or person-to-person interaction, the difference in age notwithstanding.

But for the transplant, assimilation and Americanization, both of which can be viewed as necessary processes of blending, become some of those necessary occurrences that have a way of systematically undermining and gradually negating some of the admirable qualities of his previous culture. The one outstanding aspect of some of these other cultures, as claimed by their supporters, is that these cultures have lived through time and have a history that predates the American culture. Theirs is seen as not only having endured through the test of time but also has something akin to salubrity in its ability to curb impertinence and the occasional disruption of peaceful coexistence from youthful impetuosity.

Whereas these other cultures laud their historical and communal values, the American system touts its youthful and practical approach to life. It seeks to elevate the individual, big or small, to the level of being equal—the factor of equality actualized by the instance of his personhood. This process also admits and highlights, in substrate, the American cultural adherence to individualism. And, of course, as its proponents would argue, the American system fits the moment and suits the moment. It flows with the demands of the present-day rush for life and encapsulates the change and implications of change in human interactions. This system, it is believed, anticipates and accommodates the inadequacy and inability of older systems to effectively address some present-day human needs. Ultimately, the American system addresses the generality of humanity in its openness and forward-looking approach.

The proponents of the superiority of older cultures, however, have been known to counter with the claim that the American system is inherently transient and, in its transiency, loses sight of important historical antecedents that would otherwise provide the stopgap to prevent the loss of substance in a system permanently on a fast track.

At this point, you are essentially no longer a transplant as such but part of the vegetation or soil, whichever fits your mold; and your perhaps humble beginnings in the old country have steadily faded into the permanence of the past. Your person is now molded into a different human, whose perspectives on life and its blessings and tragedies have changed in accordance with the experiences you've lived in America. And the one sure thing about America and the influence of its culture on the individual is that it leaves little or no room for late-stage adjustments. You are either very Americanized and wearing the garb pointedly on your person, or you choose to straddle between the two very different mental dispositions—the other one being when, as a settled transplant, you seek to find a middle point in which you strive to always convince yourself that living here forever has not really changed you. In this instance, you are quick to claim, like everyone else, the American heritage along with both the real and the perceived blessings that come with it, particularly in times when there is something to be gained from this posture. But in different instances when the situation appears to condemn the American way and question the fundamental basis of the culture, you play down any sign of being Americanized and seek to emphasize your allegiance to your previous culture. But in substance, as an individual who's decidedly chosen to live in America, you are just as American as the next fellow who feels he has no allegiance to any other heritage besides the American; and your pretense becomes only an attempted denial of the obvious. But America being what it is, even this behavior could still find a host of admirers. As the proponents of the American system would say, that is yet another beauty of the culture, which accommodates and protects every individual, irrespective of his allegiance to the system, or the pretense thereof.

In your quiet moments, assuming you've found a way to create some in your daily life, like most individuals, you are inclined to want to take stock of your acquisitions and successes so far. You size up your place in the community and analyze the status of your own personal culture. You take inventory of your toys and assess the effort and energy you've expended so far.

By taking such inventory, you come full circle to the true value of whatever you've strived for since you relocated and you also come face-to-face with that which now is clearly a perceived value. You begin to seek meaning and justification for why you spent so much energy chasing what now seems essentially unimportant in the sphere of the totality of your life. And as you do this, the meaninglessness of some of your endeavors becomes so apparent that you wonder what motivated your actions in the first place. But a further careful analysis may help to put things in a much clearer perspective.

Things become clearer when considered in line with the whole thing American, which is further blessed by the whole thing human. And this becomes a dilemma encountered by everyone, including your neighbor, who appears to have no regrets and seems very comfortable with whatever fortune he wallows in. And, yes, this seemingly very happy neighbor, the people would whisper to you, has his moments as well. And you can trust them on this because you only need to watch as time and trouble begin to peel off the facade and the otherwise happy fellow vanishes behind a veil of unmistakable despondency. And incidentally, some of these folks have been known to never resurface from their misery.

And this, the traveler entertains, presents as a very human tragedy that underscores the very fragile nature of the human mind.

Could this instance of fragility be eliminated from the sphere of humanity? he wonders.

> And as it is;
> There is no mystery about everything,
> But everything mystery about *nothing*.

And then the traveler stops; he is not intending to stop permanently and end his travels. He stops to consider the situations and instances that typify the human experience. It may not necessarily be a

IKE C. UDEH

damned-if-you-do-and-damned-if-don't situation, but something about it seems hopelessly designed with tragedy as a critical component. But there is beauty as he admits, but then also the very attractive aspect of an object's beauty derives its nature from the novelty and brevity of its nature.

But of necessity, you continue to do all you can to live; and as you live, you take stock of your inventory. Perhaps you've been quite successful in your adopted society. You acquired the toys, and you found a footing. You became transformed and adopted a personality fitting and proper for the system, and you developed a personal style with a slightly hostile and combative edge precisely tailored for a dog-eat-dog society. But in your moment of quiet reassessment, particularly at this late stage of your stay in America, you wonder, as an individual, if it all really makes sense, or does it all seem sensible because the culture has taught you how to endow every one of your endeavors with the substance of meaning and sensibility? You wonder if it all endures. And no sooner you begin to find concrete meaning for it all than a nascent sense of true substance begins to gnaw at your emotions. And as you, of necessity, look at your endeavors from your very American perspective, you are pointed to the transiency including the ephemerality necessarily inherent in the whole enterprise.

And here, the traveler hesitates to embark on the arduous task of getting out of this; or rather, he attempts to sway his mind and thinking away from this aspect of the experience. Perhaps it's not simply the ephemeral nature of most human activities that he would rather not bother to explore but also the process of such exploration, which, by its very nature, seems to go nowhere and ends nowhere. And besides, are there any human doings that do not pass? But he appreciates the apparent fact that as humans settle themselves in one locale, they in time build themselves a community; and in time, this community is adorned with objects that give it a sense of permanence. As for this angle of human enterprise, it appears, from the traveler's perspective, such permanence is only an attempt at a forever thing, which beacons at true eternity.

But you are quite probably settled in your new locale, albeit a settled person with a unique foreign perspective currently reinterpreted through the American culture; the road to success, including personal wellbeing in America, may have gone through some very interesting but pleasant tracks, or it probably ran through so many difficult issues and difficult experiences that you could consider yours a pyrrhic victory. But by whichever measure you analyze the results of your endeavors, the ultimate question you ask yourself is still the same: how has it affected your life? The possible difference in interpretation here then becomes distinctions in status. Obviously, if you are doing your analysis from a materially successful standpoint, some of the headaches you encountered on the way to success could be mitigated by the apparent mental gratification derived from the perception that, whatever be the situation, you are quite prepared to take care of things or at least marshal the necessary forces to deal with any problems.

But if your situation is not exactly a mirror of the financial or other success you'd envisaged, your analysis of your endeavors may be tempered by a retrospection that seems to point to other ways you could have done things or some other endeavor that could have been more gratifying and, perhaps, more lucrative. Your feeling about the results of your endeavors so far would not only be dissatisfying but also undermined by the uncertainty of your pecuniary handicap.

In spite of a sensible approach to taking stock of your efforts and despite the honesty involved in your analysis, the end result of all you've done still centers on the *dollar* and its ever-present and far-reaching implications. And this is when it really dawns on you more than it ever did as an individual that, in America, the sum total of your net worth as a person is ultimately determined by the totality of your material success and placed in its social context according to your ethnicity. This is a very American cultural trait, and that's why a wealthy and financially loaded black person or other minority can very often be greeted in a posh hotel with "You looking for something" or "Sir, can I help you with something?" The word *sir* pointedly spat in his face to take the place of "Your kind is not really wanted around here."

On the contrary, a nonminority could walk into the same hotel looking not totally raggedy but sort of out of place, as strongly suggested by his garb; and everyone, including the manager, is on his feet to genuinely offer *service*.

And you don't really condemn the whole culture for this remarkable attribute. Of course not, especially when you remember that the discriminating character or characters at the hotel or spa could be a minority or just as black as the potential guest across the desk. After such an experience, you, as a minority transplant in America, may begin to see why the finger of blame truly points to everyone, irrespective of his type and place in the society.

And as he ponders this aspect of the human nature, the traveler wonders what motivates a person to seek to insult and/or abuse others simply to gain an apparent satisfaction of one-up-man-ship. This unfortunate aspect of the human nature, he reasons, is not really limited to any one particular ethnic group; it is rather disconcerting, that this too becomes yet another blemish on the human nature. The traveler also laments the fact that this aspect of the human nature also factors into a person's approach to seeking and managing money; it is, apparently, a negative that seems so very pronounced it becomes an inherent blemish, rather difficult to avoid and ineluctable in its grasp.

And thus, the traveler suspects that, in substance, for the individual in America, or, practically, any human society, the ultimate question becomes: How do you manage money so your money does not begin to manage you? The significance of this question is that, in spite of your woes and miseries or despite your well-placed financial strength, picking up a dollar or two might satiate a personal yearning momentarily but could still leave you empty inside and searching for something you feel could truly satisfy a rather personal emotional need.

And here's where, at times, those folks with the *word* will tell you that the end of your search lies in believing in their preaching and sermons.

But you wonder how anyone can truly help you find any viable answers when that same preacher, as well as others, are looking to make a dollar or two off you. And just as you proceed to think further about some of these present-day messiahs, you take another look at the dollar in your pocket, perhaps your very last, and it still poignantly proclaims In God We Trust.

Now you realize, after a more critical look at this fundamental element of social hierarchy that constantly tells you and everyone else about this all-encompassing trust in God, could be suspect.

You begin to feel a trifle more deflated in spirit as you consider the fact that that same item—the dollar that sparks so much hate, spills so much blood, and causes so much pain—is the only universal thing that wears an exceptionally unique slogan on its face. To make things more complicated, the dollar, which remains the very soul of Americanism, employs the God slogan to boost the symbolism implied by its presence and enhance any claims made by its mention. Even in its absence, in almost all areas of human intercourse, the dollar invokes might and power and the promise of transforming abstract sentiments into the reality of material comfort.

It was a remarkable instance of foresight to decide to place this unique slogan on the dollar. One very daring quality of this God slogan is that it remains a very powerful force behind the perceived need for America to continue to be the leader among the nations. Interestingly, while everyone else's currency is struggling to sustain its worth, the dollar, with its God slogan, stands as the ultimate guarantee of material human comfort. Even in its rather difficult days when America is steeped in deep financial deficits, the dollar still commands the ultimate respect. It is as if while other currencies are struggling for respect and global recognition, the dollar appears to rest quite comfortably in its own sphere and is only vying with itself for a permanence in divine essence.

Like all human elements of perceived essential materialism, the American dollar stakes its claims with every possible tool at its disposal and some of these tools can be very unkind and brutal.

But being a manmade object, in this case *money*, the marriage of the word God with this ultrahuman object becomes an exceedingly interesting item for debate. Seen from a purely American perspective, this God slogan on the dollar comes with a touch of kindness stemming from a very staunch belief in God as the one and only force that touches all of humanity in its unique instance of true universality.

According to its opponents, however, this strange marriage is the height of blasphemy, predicated on the platform of pretentious American arrogance.

At this point, you are very free to choose your side. As for this writer, there is a rather strong inclination that urges the spread of a few dollars and doing the debate later.

Perhaps the one very disconcerting factor about the dollar—and, incidentally, every other human money or its substitute thereof—is that at the same time it is utilized to provide some of the very basics in a person's life, it could also be used as a very strong instrument for the destruction of that same person's life.

And now, you really wonder, in exactly what God do we trust?

Perhaps, as a transplant in America, you've scored big and found riches. You count your blessings or curses, depending on what your money makes you do. You increase the effort and the drive for more riches because you know only too well that a little mishap could leave you empty.

But if yours has been a series of misses and ill luck, you work hard to find reasons for your misfortune and fervently hope that a more effortful approach will lead you to fortune. As you toil at your new endeavor, you may notice the seemingly slower passage of time—as if designed by nature to prolong the period of your destitution. This is when you begin to count the moments and hope that your success is just around the corner.

And as the moments pass, a somewhat neutral mental disposition may touch your sense of reality. You realize it's all a very American instance, in a very American scene. It's the limit of the sky, perceived or real. It's abundance, whether accessible in its concrescence or simply promised and beyond reach in its abstraction. It is wealth and riches tangible in your grasp or manifestly existent only as a make believe. It is beauty, truly natural or elegantly objectified to sustain the illusion of immortality, or simply carved into place to aid the body in its pretense at youth. It is the hoot and holler, whether sincere and deemed to cheer a good deed or simply a put-on intended to boost your image and diminish your neighbor's presence.

And, yes, it is also a very American thing that encourages you to question and investigate whatever life or your neighbor throws at you. In substance, this process of questioning, apparently, nudges you closer to a more effective sense of safety. But incidentally, it also nudges your mind toward enlightenment and wraps your sentiments with the knowledge that it is a uniquely American experience in which, apparently, the one and only constant is the dollar in its seductive presence, constantly proclaiming In God We Trust.

And then it dawns on the traveler, trusting in God encompasses a variety of human experiences; and this trust is couched on a staunch belief in God, which is often informed by the individual's religious inclinations. But could he appreciate that when there is wholesome, unmitigated trust, the trustee entrusts his person and, as always, the essence of his being to the trusted God or force? And this becomes a question that drags into a continuous spell of nonanswer!

The traveler then proceeds to take in the entire situation, including the totality of the experience. Nonetheless, he wonders if in the ultimate it has been a pleasurable experience; but there is little need to wonder since every experience is a learning process and the beauty of an experience lies in the knowledge gained including the substance, both mental and material derived from it.

As he takes in the whole picture, the traveler recalls that you've been a new arrival; you've been at the starting point of the ladder of success. You then struggled and toiled at your chosen occupation and worked your way to your current position. And now, it appears, you see yourself in the mix of the American social melting pot, your precise position in this mix never clearly defined but forever egged on by the system's tantalizing promise, and always teased by the seductive nuance and whisper of material success. You have a bag full of toys and a head bashed and strained by the system's uncompromising demands. You have a mind loaded with experience, often utilized to tend a bodily presence weather-beaten and issue laden.

It was a few words, then a story, news of betterment, and a tale of grandeur—about this new land, whose superlatively designed social structure beckoned—and you responded. Your affirmative response now finds you at this point, in this moment of your relocation to America. And the only true constant still remains the slogan on the dollar in your possession. Yet, you know how quickly this dollar can go and will certainly go. You realize so very well how definite and imminent its departure is. You fear the emptiness that would be left by this departure since the life and scene remind you of the need to find another in order to guarantee the continuum that ensures your subsistence.

So you plan a brief rest, with a catnap, before a return to the obvious and perennial—a routinized chase for this dollar, a critical element of subsistence. And as you wake up and find your cue, you step out into

The drift,
And—
The flow,
Of—
Insouciant air;
The masses,
Of humanity;
Otherwise known,
As—
A faceless crowd;
The klunk,
And—
The clatter,
Of automobile;
The funk,
And—
The clutter,
Of dislocation—
All woven,
Into the rush,
And the chatter,
Of –
Talkative heads.

And this maddening rush of human traffic is so typical of your daily trip to work that you call it the rush hour, a term that suggests permanence.

And then, there is the traveler, not exactly isolated or removed from the goings-on but seemingly present in a very nonpresent, rather shifting void.

Perhaps there is no mystery about his presence, but apparently, there is no presence within or without the scene.

At this juncture, the traveler grasps the enormity of the stress and the drag such lifestyle puts on the individual; then, he considers the inescapable reason for which people find it necessary to place so much demand on themselves: they have to earn a living. But then, the traveler recalls, with humans, chasing the dollar for survival is one thing—what the dollar makes some do is another. He ruminates about the being, his resolve, his mental strength; then, he embarks on a mental debate regarding the apparent preordained fallibility of the human creature. It would seem evident based on this instance that the human person is doomed and trapped in an inadmirable situation from which he could not extricate himself. The traveler wonders if there is something about money, something not quite commendable that breaks a person's resolve. In an apparent acquiescence, he laments what seems like an inherent corruptibility of the human essence. But, he admits, there is a reason for the constant chase for the dollar and something about this chase makes it seem perennial.

You remain very aware, as always, that this perennial chase for the dollar, which you so badly need in order to live in America, is a lifelong enterprise. And when the bills come due, as they surely will, you empty your pockets to stop the creditors and satisfy the needs of dependents. You dare not fail or let a lapse in judgment prevent you from doing this; otherwise, you lose your footing and begin to drown in the black hole of the system's precipice of economic disaster.

And, no, you have no one to rescue you. You have no one to stop his own chase and shoulder the responsibility of your financial rescue. You only have yourself, your troubles, and a worried mind, now steadily whispering into your ears, "Oh yes, this is America, and this is the process!"

ABOUT THE AUTHOR

H ARVARD EDUCATION, TETERBORO School of Aeronautics, lives in Silicon Valley, California.

Printed in the United States
By Bookmasters